AI-CADEMIA: A SIMPLIFIED GUIDE TO AI FOR EDUCATORS

NAVIGATE DIGITAL-AGE TEACHING, MASTER FUNDAMENTALS, STREAMLINE INSTRUCTION, AND ELEVATE STUDENT EXPERIENCE IN THE CLASSROOM OR AT HOME

TEACH WISE PUBLICATIONS

CONTENTS

Introduction	vii
1. DEBUNKING THE AI MYTHOLOGY	1
Common Misconceptions About AI	1
The Reality of AI in Modern Classrooms	4
User-Friendly AI Platforms Designed for Educators	7
AI's Role in Streamlining Administrative Tasks, Personalized Learning, and More	9
Checkpoint	11
2. NAVIGATING THE ETHICS OF AI IN THE CLASSROOM	13
Ethical Dilemmas and Considerations	13
Unveiling the Potential of Biases in AI Algorithms	15
AI's Impact on Holistic Education in the Standardized Testing Era	19
The Risk of Over-Reliance on Technology	20
Strategies for Ensuring Data Privacy	21
AI Tool Ethical Consideration Checklist for Educators	25
3. TAILOR-MADE TEACHING—AI'S ROLE IN PERSONALIZED LEARNING	28
The Mechanics of Personalized AI-Driven Learning	28
Revolutionizing Assessments: AI's Adaptive Quiz and Assignment Evolution	30
AI Predictive Abilities	31
Real-World Applications	32
AI in Education: Reflect, Predict, and Collaborate	36
4. ENGAGING MINDS—AI'S ROLE IN ELEVATING STUDENT ENGAGEMENT	39
AI-Driven Tools and Strategies for Engagement	39
Measuring the Success of AI Tools	45
Leveraging AI Analytics for Enhanced Student Engagement	46
Decoding Observational Data in the Classroom	48
AI Revolution in Education: Transforming Learning Landscapes in New Zealand and Beyond	49
Key Takeaways	51

5. STREAMLINING THE CLASSROOM—A TEACHER'S
   GUIDE TO AI EFFICIENCY ... 54
   The Era of Smart Classrooms ... 55
   Efficient Classroom Management With AI ... 58
   Time-Saving AI Applications for Educators ... 59
   Teachers Harnessing the Power of AI ... 62
   Key Takeaways ... 63

6. SURFING THE AI WAVE—STAYING ABREAST OF AI
   DEVELOPMENTS ... 65
   Methods to Keep Up with AI Advancements ... 65
   A Checklist for You ... 73

7. SEIZING THE FUTURE—PREPARING FOR AN AI-
   INFUSED EDUCATION LANDSCAPE ... 75
   The Long-Term Vision of AI in Education ... 75
   Revolutionizing Education With AI: Personalized
   Learning, Accessibility, and Global Impact ... 77
   Preparation Strategies for Educators ... 78
   Tech-Infused Classrooms: A Futuristic Blend of Learning
   and Innovation ... 80
   Sketching the Future of AI-Enhanced Learning ... 82

8. HOMESCHOOLING IN THE AGE OF AI—UNLEASHING
   THE POWER OF PERSONALIZED LEARNING ... 84
   Benefits of AI in Homeschooling Environments ... 84
   Tools and Strategies Tailored for Homeschool Educators ... 89
   Interactive Decision Pathway: Personalized AI Learning
   for Your Students ... 94
   Key Takeaways ... 96
   Putting Ideas into Action ... 97

9. THE ART OF AI PROMPTS—A CONVERSATION
   STARTER ... 98
   AI Prompts ... 98
   A Step-By-Step Guide for Creating Effective Prompts ... 101
   Unlocking the Potential: 100 AI Prompts for Educational
   Enrichment ... 103
   Crafting Engaging AI Prompts for Students ... 110
   Interactive Element: Crafting Effective ChatGPT Prompts ... 111

10. AI AND THE HUMAN TOUCH—STRIKING A BALANCE
    IN THE CLASSROOM   113
    The Integral Role of Human Emotion and Intuition in
    Education   113
    Strategies to Ensure AI Remains a Tool, not a
    Replacement   116
    Balancing AI and Human Intervention Worksheet   117

    Leading the Way in AI Education   119
    Conclusion   123
    Bibliography   127
    About the Author   131

© **Copyright 2023 - All rights reserved.**

The content contained within this book may not be reproduced, duplicated, or transmitted without direct written permission from the author or the publisher.

Under no circumstances will any blame or legal responsibility be held against the publisher or author for any damages, reparation, or monetary loss due to the information contained within this book, either directly or indirectly.

Legal Notice:

This book is copyright-protected. It is only for personal use. You cannot amend, distribute, sell, use, quote or paraphrase any part, or the content within this book, without the consent of the author or publisher.

Disclaimer Notice:

Please note the information contained within this document is for educational and entertainment purposes only. All effort has been executed to present accurate, up to date, reliable, complete information. No warranties of any kind are declared or implied. Readers acknowledge that the author is not engaged in the rendering of legal, financial, medical or professional advice. The content within this book has been derived from various sources. Please consult a licensed professional before attempting any techniques outlined in this book.

By reading this document, the reader agrees that under no circumstances is the author responsible for any losses, direct or indirect, that are incurred as a result of the use of the information contained within this document, including, but not limited to, errors, omissions, or inaccuracies.

INTRODUCTION

Remember the days when "smart classrooms" meant having a projector? A time when the height of technological sophistication in education was the satisfying hum of an overhead projector bulb warming up. Fast forward to today. Imagine a classroom where lessons aren't just taught; they are tailor-made in real time to suit each student's unique learning journey. Imagine questions answered before they're even asked, and the "teacher's pet" isn't a student sitting in the front row but a piece of software quietly orchestrating the symphony of learning. Welcome to the future of education.

You may be grappling with the idea of artificial intelligence (AI) as an abstract concept, finding it difficult to grasp its concrete relevance in your classroom. Imagine the weight of this uncertainty—how it tugs at your desire to provide the best for your students. We understand. The overwhelm that comes with the rapid pace of technological advancements, the nagging fear of being left behind, or the feeling of inadequacy in the face of AI's complexity—we are right there with you. It is like trying to catch a train that is already speeding down the tracks.

There are ethical conundrums everywhere you look. Concerns around student autonomy, data privacy, and the thin line separating creativity and accountability are not just hypothetical; they are actual worries that cross your mind when you consider using AI in your teaching methods.

Then, there is the real worry that adopting AI will weaken the human connection, which is the vital thread that runs through both successful teaching and learning. Finding a balance becomes a never-ending tightrope walk, making you wonder if you are balancing the technological and human aspects of education fairly. You feel like you are on the verge of becoming obsolete if you do not keep up with the times. We know you want to be that cutting-edge, dynamic teacher, but the rate of change can be daunting.

Integrating AI into existing teaching strategies adds another layer of complexity. How do you seamlessly blend the traditional with the technological? The struggle is real, and we understand the challenges you face in finding that sweet spot.

And those fears about AI potentially replacing teachers—it's not just a passing thought. It's a concern rooted in a genuine passion for the craft of teaching, a fear that the very essence of what you do might be overshadowed or, worse, rendered obsolete.

Some of you may harbor doubts about the effectiveness of AI in improving learning outcomes. It's not skepticism for skepticism's sake; it's a yearning for evidence that what you integrate into your classroom genuinely benefits your students.

Let's pause for a moment and reflect on the catalyst—the spark that led you to the doorstep of *AI-cademia*. It's not just about the intriguing title or the promise of unraveling the mysteries of AI. It's something more personal, isn't it?

Maybe it was that moment when you looked around your classroom and realized the landscape of education was shifting. The projector, once the pinnacle of technological sophistication, suddenly seemed quaint. Perhaps it was the realization that to truly connect with your students, to meet their ever-evolving needs, you needed to understand this new player in the game—artificial intelligence.

It could be the quiet concern that nudged you to explore AI's potential. The fear of being left behind, the relentless pace of change that whispers in your ear, urging you to catch up. You're not just an observer; you're a participant in the evolution of education, and the realization hit that AI is not a distant concept—it's here, in your classroom, shaping the way you teach and the way your students learn.

Maybe you bought this book because you're standing at the crossroads of tradition and innovation. The realization that the future of education isn't just a concept—it's a reality waiting for you to embrace it. It's that desire to not just keep up with the wave of AI developments but to ride it confidently, knowing you're equipped to steer the course.

Was it the late-night reflection on your teaching methods, a quest for that missing piece that could elevate student engagement? The longing for tools that go beyond the traditional that can captivate minds and make learning an adventure.

Perhaps the catalyst was the pressure, the undeniable push to adapt and stay relevant. The awareness that the classroom is transforming, and to be the best educator you can be, you need to understand not just the "what" but the "why" of AI in education.

For some, it could be the curiosity about personalized learning, a desire to tailor your teaching methods to suit the unique needs of each student. To turn the one-size-fits-all approach into a customized, dynamic educational experience.

Or was it the quiet worry about the potential loss of the human touch—the essence of teaching that makes education not just a transfer of knowledge but a deeply personal connection? Balancing technology and humanity in a way that enhances, not diminishes, the educational experience.

Whatever the catalyst, we get it. We understand where you are in your journey—the challenges, the fears, the aspirations. *"AI-cademia"* is a companion on this transformative adventure, a guide through the realm of AI in education.

Embarking on the journey through *"AI-cademia"* isn't just about flipping pages; it's about unlocking a treasure trove of benefits tailored just for you:

- **Streamlined understanding:** Dive into the world of AI without drowning in confusing terms. We're breaking down the complex stuff into bite-sized, actionable insights made just for you. No tech jargon here—just a straightforward guide to get your head around AI.
- **Ethics at the forefront:** Ever feel like you're wading through a sea of articles just to get the lowdown on AI ethics? We've got your back. This book is your one-stop shop for a deep dive into the ethical side of AI in education. Save your sanity and get the full picture in one go.
- **Future-proof strategies:** Stay ahead of the game without needing a crystal ball. We're not just talking about today's AI; we're handing you the keys to tomorrow's trends. Skip the endless research, and let's get you future-proofed, shall we?
- **Diverse applications:** Whether you're rocking a K-12 classroom, navigating university lectures, or mastering the homeschooling game, we've got AI strategies tailored just for you. No more trying to fit a square peg into a round hole—save time and get strategies that actually match your teaching vibes.
- **Engagement amplified:** Tired of trial and error to boost student engagement? We hear you. Discover tried-and-true techniques to make your classroom buzz with energy. Say goodbye to guessing games and hello to strategies that really work.
- **Efficiency maximized:** Integrating AI shouldn't feel like climbing Mount Everest. Let's keep it simple. Learn how to weave AI seamlessly into your teaching methods. No stress, no steep learning curves—just more effective lessons without the headache.
- **Personalized learning:** Want to be the superhero of personalized learning without spending eons on assessments? Say no more. We'll show you how to use AI to tailor your teaching to each student's unique needs. More personalized learning, less time-consuming guesswork.
- **Stay updated:** Scanning the tech horizon for the latest AI developments sounds exhausting, right? Let us save you the trouble. This book is your shortcut to staying in the loop. Get the updates without the constant tech-hunting hustle.

AI stands poised to revolutionize the education sector, offering a transformative array of benefits. The key lies in empowering educators with the knowledge and strategies needed to leverage this technology effectively.

AI's impact is far-reaching, from tailoring lesson plans through personalized learning to adapting in real-time with adaptive learning platforms, identifying knowledge gaps, and providing instant feedback.

Virtual tutors powered by AI can offer continuous support, while automated administrative tasks free up teachers to focus on instruction and student interaction. Beyond the classroom, AI-driven language translation tools break down communication barriers, fostering collaboration among students and educators with diverse linguistic backgrounds.

Equipping students with a basic understanding of AI is paramount for developing digital literacy and critical thinking skills and preparing them for future academic and career success. Learning about AI not only encourages ethical engagement but also positions students to navigate the evolving job market, where AI skills are increasingly in demand.

Moreover, AI education is a tool for addressing diversity, equity, and inclusion, ensuring underrepresented student populations have access to the skills needed for success in technology and related fields. Closing opportunity gaps, fostering innovation, and empowering communities for positive change are integral outcomes of integrating AI education into the educational landscape (George, 2023).

The roles of AI in education, such as personalizing education, generating smart content, automating tasks, providing tutoring, and ensuring access for students with special needs, collectively contribute to a richer and more inclusive learning experience (Plitnichenko, 2020).

Teach Wise Publications assumes the role of an authority in guiding educators through the realms of AI in education. With a mission centered on empowering educators with the tools, insights, and resources to harness AI's potential in the classroom, Teach Wise Publications embodies a commitment to bridging the gap between pedagogy and artificial intelligence.

The organization is driven by the belief that educators must be equipped not only with knowledge but also with practical strategies to seamlessly integrate AI into the educational landscape. Our expertise lies in demystifying complex AI concepts, ensuring they are comprehensible and actionable for educators. Through this commitment, we emerge as a trusted guide, providing a unique blend of technical know-how, ethical considerations, and forward-thinking insights to usher educators confidently into the AI-enhanced future of education.

In the pages of this book, you won't find just another tech manual. Instead, you'll discover a companion that empathizes with the overwhelm of technological advancements, the uncertainty about AI's relevance, and the genuine desire to enhance your teaching methods without losing the human touch.

"AI-cademia" is not about overwhelming you with jargon; it's about streamlining your understanding of AI in a way that resonates with educators like yourself. From personalized learning to adaptive strategies, we've got practical shortcuts to save you time and energy, making AI not just accessible but genuinely beneficial for your teaching journey.

Whether you're in K-12, higher ed, or navigating the world of homeschooling, this book is crafted with your unique needs in mind. It's not a one-size-fits-all approach; it's a tailored resource designed to fit seamlessly into your teaching environment.

As you flip through these pages, envision a future where you're not just keeping up with AI developments but confidently leading the way. Picture a classroom where engagement is amplified, lessons are more efficient, and the power of AI enhances rather than hinders the art of education.

1

DEBUNKING THE AI MYTHOLOGY

Contrary to popular belief, AI has existed in educational settings for over two decades (Guan et al., 2020). Long before the buzzwords echoed in academic conferences and webinars, AI was orchestrating a silent symphony behind the scenes, enhancing our classrooms in ways we might not have even realized.

As we embark on this chapter's journey, let's unravel the rich fabric of AI's presence in education. It's not a recent arrival; it's a seasoned aspect that has gracefully evolved alongside the chalkboards and textbooks, adapting to the nuances of each educational era. Let's shatter some myths that might be lingering in our minds like mischievous phantoms.

Common Misconceptions About AI

In our exploration of the AI landscape, it's crucial to debunk some common misconceptions that might be casting shadows on the true potential of AI in education.

Misconception 1: AI Can Replace Educators

One prevalent myth is that AI aims to replace educators, painting a dystopian picture of classrooms devoid of human interaction. The reality, however, is far from this misconception. AI is not here to replace educators; instead, it complements and enhances their roles. It serves as a powerful tool, offering support in various aspects of teaching, from personalized lesson planning to real-time feedback. In the recent article "The Rise of Education and AI: Will Robots Replace Teachers?" (Santosh K, 2023), the author has this to say about it: "While AI has the potential to revolutionize the education industry, it is unlikely that robots will completely replace teachers. Teachers provide a personal touch that AI cannot replace, and they bring creativity, passion, and emotional support to the classroom."

Misconception 2: Implementing AI Requires Significant Technical Expertise

Another misconception that looms large is the belief that implementing AI in education demands an abundance of technical expertise. When individuals encounter the term AI, the immediate association tends to be with complexity, often conjuring the perception that it requires a specialized skill set to navigate. The truth is that AI tools are becoming increasingly user-friendly and designed to be accessible to educators with varying levels of technical proficiency. Modern AI applications often come with intuitive interfaces, allowing educators to integrate AI into their teaching methods without being IT experts. Demystifying this myth empowers educators to explore and adopt AI tools with confidence, knowing that technical prowess is not a prerequisite.

Misconception 3: AI Is Only for Tech-Oriented Subjects or Advanced Students

A common misperception suggests that AI is reserved for tech-oriented subjects or advanced students, excluding other disciplines or learners. However, AI's versatility extends beyond the realms of science and technology. AI has permeated every facet of education, breaking free from the confines of the scientific wing. Its application is no longer limited; instead, it spans diverse subjects, enriching the learning experience in the humanities, arts, and beyond.

Furthermore, AI tools can be tailored to accommodate students at various skill levels, making them inclusive rather than exclusive. By dispelling this myth, educators can embrace the broad applicability of

AI, unlocking its potential for diverse subjects and catering to the needs of all students.

Misconception 4: AI Will Replace All Human Jobs

A common fear surrounding AI is the belief that it will replace all human jobs, rendering human workers obsolete. In reality, while AI can automate specific tasks, it also opens avenues for new job opportunities. AI is a tool to enhance human capabilities, not a complete replacement. Understanding this dispels the notion of an impending job apocalypse, fostering a more nuanced view of AI's impact on employment.

Misconception 5: AI Is Infallible and Unbiased

There's a misconception that AI, being a machine, is inherently infallible and unbiased. However, AI systems are created and trained by humans, which means they can inherit human biases. Recognizing this is crucial to ensuring that AI is developed and implemented with ethical considerations, avoiding the perpetuation of biases in decision-making processes.

Misconception 6: AI Can Understand and Experience Human Emotions

While AI can analyze patterns and respond to specific cues, it doesn't truly understand or experience human emotions. Emotional intelligence remains a unique human trait. AI's ability to recognize emotions is based on data and algorithms, lacking the depth of genuine human emotional understanding. Clarifying this misconception prevents unrealistic expectations about AI's capacity for emotional engagement.

Misconception 7: AI Will Inevitably Become Sentient and Surpass Human Intelligence

There's a futuristic notion that AI will inevitably evolve into sentient beings, surpassing human intelligence. However, achieving true sentience remains a theoretical and ethical challenge. AI, as we currently know it, lacks consciousness and self-awareness. Acknowledging this dispels the notion of an imminent AI uprising, allowing for a more realistic and responsible approach to its development.

Misconception 8: AI Works Like the Human Brain

Contrary to the belief that AI operates similarly to the human brain, the two function quite differently. While AI excels at processing vast amounts of data quickly, it lacks the nuanced, contextual understanding that human cognition possesses. Understanding this distinction is essential for appreciating the unique strengths and limitations of both AI and human intelligence.

Misconception 9: AI Can Solve Any Problem

There's a misconception that AI is an all-encompassing problem-solving tool. While AI can excel in specific domains, it doesn't possess a universal problem-solving capability. The effectiveness of AI depends on factors like data quality, algorithm design, and problem complexity. Clarifying this misconception encourages a more realistic view of AI's applicability and encourages thoughtful consideration of its implementation (Digital Learning Institute, 2023).

Now, educators, as you embark on this AI-infused journey, it is crucial to remember that you are the architects of the future of education. Embrace AI as a tool for enhancement, a partner in innovation, and a facilitator of personalized, inclusive learning experiences.

The Reality of AI in Modern Classrooms

As we have already agreed, in the modern classroom, AI isn't a distant entity; it's an integral part of the educational ecosystem. It's the ally that personalizes learning, creates efficient study tools, offers versatile assessments, and facilitates direct interaction.

AI as a Supplementary Tool Enhancing Teaching Methods

Consider AI as your reliable teaching assistant, a tool designed to work in tandem with you, not replace you. The reality is that personalization reaches its peak when AI tailors lessons based on individual learning styles. Take Jenny, a high school student struggling with algebra. With AI, she receives personalized exercises and immediate feedback, directly impacting her learning experience.

This isn't a distant idea; it's happening now and reshaping how we address diverse student needs. AI recognizes specific challenges and adjusts its approach accordingly. In your classroom, AI is a practical force, not a far-off concept. It's working alongside you, adapting to students' unique requirements, and providing real-time support.

Imagine the shift in dynamics as students receive tailored assistance, progressing at their own pace. This is the reality of AI, not as a fanciful notion but as a tool actively transforming education. In your hands, AI becomes an essential ally, understanding and enhancing the educational journey without replacing the human touch.

Personalization at Its Best

In the realm of personalized learning, AI serves as a pivotal tool, addressing the diverse needs of students in a way that conventional methods often struggle to achieve. Recognizing the urgency for personalized learning paths, AI tools step in to create tailored educational experiences, aligning with individual strengths, weaknesses, and preferences.

As educators, it is incumbent upon us to recognize the diverse learning styles of our students. While this is feasible, and many teachers have been doing so over the years, the challenge lies in how to assist each individual student. Let's consider a scenario: You are a calculus teacher managing two different classes with a total of 120 students. Indeed, it's possible to categorize your students based on their learning rates and styles, but it requires a considerable amount of effort and time to determine the most effective strategy for each student. This is where AI becomes invaluable. It does not replace you; instead, it significantly streamlines your job, making it much more manageable. Take Alex, a visual learner who finds engagement through interactive content. AI goes beyond mere identification; it comprehends Alex's learning style. AI is able to create lessons that resonate with Alex's preferences, utilizing engaging visuals to simplify complex concepts. The outcome is transformative—an empowered student who not only comprehends but masters subjects through a personalized touch.

This isn't a theoretical concept but a practical application that is reshaping education. AI doesn't just benefit students; it becomes a priceless asset for teachers as well. Through sophisticated algorithms, AI analyzes student data, offering teachers profound insights into performance, engagement levels, and overall progress. Imagine a scenario where teachers receive real-time information pinpointing areas where students struggle. Armed with this knowledge, they can dynamically adjust their teaching methods, tailoring the curriculum to meet the evolving needs of their students.

The impact is clear: a more responsive, adaptable education system where both students and teachers benefit from the precision and insights that AI brings to the learning environment. It's not about replacing the human touch; it's about leveraging technology to enhance and personalize education for the benefit of all.

Efficient and Engaging Notes Creation

When we speak of note creation, traditional transcription tools have long been the norm, capable of converting lectures into written form but lacking the depth of understanding. However, the evolution brought by AI introduces a distinctive strength: an assistant that transcends mere transcription. Imagine a scenario where AI not only captures the spoken words but also comprehends the context, identifying key concepts and assembling pertinent information to craft comprehensive study notes.

This enhanced capability holds profound benefits for both educators and students alike. For teachers, it means the production of well-internalized content. AI doesn't just transcribe; it discerns the core concepts, aiding educators in creating rich, nuanced materials that go beyond the surface. This not only enriches the learning experience but also facilitates more effective and engaging teaching.

Now, consider a college student navigating the academic landscape. With an AI-powered note-taking assistant, the student experiences a shift from conventional transcriptions to in-depth, context-aware summaries. This transformative approach frees up their time, allowing them to delve into more profound understanding and critical thinking. It's not just about note-taking; it's about fostering a learning environment where students can truly internalize and comprehend the material.

Versatile Assessment Tools

For teachers, AI brings a game-changing way to assess students. Think of Tim, a history teacher, using AI-powered quizzes that adjust to each student's abilities. It's not the old days of the same test for everyone. Now, AI is like an intelligent tool that not only checks what students know but also customizes questions based on how each student learns. It's a modern approach, making assessments more personalized and less one-size-fits-all.

As an educator, these versatile AI-powered assessment tools become invaluable in grading students' work. The efficiency and accuracy offered by AI streamline the grading process, providing insights into student performance that go beyond traditional methods. This means more than just assigning grades; it means gaining profound insights into where students excel and where they may need additional support.

Consider this: AI doesn't just mark papers; it analyzes them with precision, offering a nuanced understanding of students' strengths and areas that require improvement. As an educator, this translates to a more informed and targeted approach to assisting your students. No longer are you confined to time-consuming grading; AI accelerates the process, freeing up your time to focus on what truly matters: guiding and supporting your students.

User-Friendly AI Platforms Designed for Educators

We understand the bias that comes with accepting AI in the realm of education, and some of it stems from a fear of how to navigate the presumed technicalities of AI. Navigating the world of artificial intelligence in education doesn't have to be daunting. These platforms serve as your companions in the journey of integrating AI into the classroom, offering seamless experiences without the need for extensive technical expertise. Whether you're a seasoned educator or just dipping your toes into the AI waters, these platforms are tailored to simplify the process, ensuring that AI becomes an accessible and beneficial tool for enhancing teaching and learning.

In the ever-evolving landscape of AI tools utilized in the classroom, we acknowledge and appreciate the vast array of innovations, from ChatGPT and Google BERT to Pi, Pictory, and Bing Chat, each of which plays a crucial role in enhancing the learning experience for students and educators alike. The contribution of these tools in closing gaps within the learning process is undeniable. However, in this exploration, we shift our focus to platforms specifically tailored to make the job of educators more seamless. These user-friendly AI platforms prioritize the unique needs of teachers, offering tools and features designed to enhance teaching practices, streamline administrative tasks, and ultimately empower educators in their amazing roles.

Squirrel AI

Squirrel AI is an adaptive learning platform that employs AI algorithms to tailor educational content to individual student needs. Educators can use this platform to provide personalized learning paths for students, ensuring that each student progresses at their own pace and receives targeted support where needed.

DreamBox

DreamBox is an AI-powered math program designed for K-8 students (students in kindergarten through 8th grade). Educators can leverage this platform to track students' progress, identify areas of struggle, and receive actionable insights to inform their teaching strategies. The adaptive nature of DreamBox ensures that students receive customized math lessons aligned with their skill levels.

Quillionz

Quillionz is an AI-powered tool that helps educators generate quiz questions and learning content quickly. Teachers can use this platform to create customized assessments, saving time on manual question creation. Quillionz uses natural language processing to understand the context and generate relevant questions for various subjects.

Knewton

Knewton is an adaptive learning platform that uses AI to personalize digital courses for students. Educators can utilize Knewton to deliver tailored content, quizzes, and assignments based on each student's learning style and performance. This platform adapts in real-time, ensuring that students receive the most relevant materials.

Edmodo

Edmodo is a social learning platform with AI features that facilitate communication and collaboration among students and educators. Teachers can use Edmodo to create a virtual classroom, share resources, and engage students in discussions. AI algorithms analyze student interactions to provide insights into engagement levels and areas that may need attention (Education World, 2013).

It's important to note that the examples provided are just a glimpse into the diverse landscape of tools available. The field of AI in education is dynamic and continually expanding, with new platforms emerging and existing ones evolving to cater to the changing needs of educators. These mentioned platforms are a starting point, showcasing the potential of AI to enhance teaching practices. However, they represent just a fraction of the rich ecosystem of AI tools at your disposal.

As the AI landscape widens, more platforms are continuously innovating, introducing improved features and personalizing the educational experience further. The world of AI in education is dynamic, and educators have a plethora of options to explore.

AI's Role in Streamlining Administrative Tasks, Personalized Learning, and More

Traditionally, the administrative side of education has been laden with labor-intensive and time-consuming processes, from student registration to record-keeping and scheduling. Enter AI, the game-changer that's revolutionizing how these tasks are handled, freeing up valuable time for administrators to focus on more strategic endeavors.

AI-powered systems seamlessly manage vast amounts of student data, not just as a record-keeping tool but as an insightful ally. These systems swiftly process and analyze data, unveiling patterns that educators can leverage for personalized learning plans. Imagine having the ability to predict future academic performance, enabling educators to tailor their approaches and enhance overall learning outcomes.

Scheduling, often a logistical puzzle, is no longer a headache. AI algorithms, taking into account teacher availability, student preferences, and classroom capacity, craft optimal timetables with efficiency. This isn't just about managing resources—it's about creating schedules that maximize student satisfaction and engagement.

Communication, a cornerstone of education, receives a tech-savvy boost from AI-powered chatbots. These virtual assistants work round the clock, providing instant responses to students' queries about course details, deadlines, and campus facilities. By handling routine questions, AI liberates administrators to delve into more complex issues, fostering a more efficient and responsive educational environment.

Security, a paramount concern, gets a high-tech upgrade. AI-powered surveillance systems vigilantly monitor campuses, identifying unusual activity and alerting authorities in real time. This proactive approach not only prevents incidents but also ensures the safety of students and staff, creating a secure and conducive learning environment (Frąckiewicz, 2023a).

Checkpoint

The following list will test what you know as regards the integration of AI in education:

- AI tools are too expensive for most schools. Myth or reality?
- AI is only beneficial for subjects related to technology and computer science. Myth or reality?
- Students require a deep understanding of technology to benefit from AI-assisted education. Myth or reality?
- AI can automatically adjust its teaching methods based on each student's learning pace. Myth or reality?
- Teachers require extensive training to implement AI tools in the classroom. Myth or reality?
- AI in education only benefits students, not educators. Myth or reality?
- Integrating AI in education compromises the personal touch and human interaction of teaching. Myth or reality?
- AI-driven platforms can potentially detect when a student is struggling with the content and needs extra help. Myth or reality?
- AI tools can't help in subjects that require creativity, like the arts and music. Myth or reality?
- Using AI for grading assignments and tests is always 100% accurate and unbiased. Myth or reality?
- AI can understand and process multiple languages, making it a useful tool for diverse classrooms. Myth or reality?

In this chapter, we unraveled the myths surrounding AI in education, dispelling misconceptions, and shedding light on the realities. From debunking the notion that AI is only for tech-oriented subjects to exploring its potential across diverse disciplines, we've navigated the landscape of AI in the classroom. Remember, AI isn't here to replace educators but to support and enhance their efforts.

As you reflect on these revelations, consider how AI can be a dynamic tool in your teaching arsenal. Personalized learning, efficient note creation, and versatile assessment tools are not just theoretical concepts but practical enhancements awaiting your exploration. Now, armed with a clearer understanding, it's time to put these ideas into action.

In the next chapter, we'll delve into a crucial aspect of AI in education—ethics. Are our students' data secure? Is using AI for grading morally right? These questions and more will be explored, providing you with insights and considerations to navigate the ethical landscape of AI in the classroom. Get ready for a thought-provoking journey as we continue our exploration of *AI-cademia.*

2

NAVIGATING THE ETHICS OF AI IN THE CLASSROOM

In 2021 alone, millions of students had their personal data exposed through educational software. It is a stark reminder of the critical need for ethical considerations in the realm of AI in education. We cannot afford to overlook the ethical implications, and in this chapter, we will navigate the complex landscape of ethics in AI.

The integration of AI is not just about technological advancements but also about safeguarding the privacy and well-being of every student. As we delve into the ethical dilemmas surrounding AI in education, you will gain insights and strategies to prioritize student data privacy and foster responsible AI integration in your classroom. Get ready to navigate the ethics of AI, where every decision counts and every data point matters.

Ethical Dilemmas and Considerations

Ethical dilemmas are those tricky situations where you find yourself caught between two conflicting moral principles, scratching your head about what the right course of action should be. Imagine this playing out in the realm of AI in your classroom.

Ethical considerations in the AI education landscape mean taking a step back and pondering the potential impact of AI on students, teachers, and the entire educational ecosystem. It is about weighing the benefits against potential harms and making choices that align with moral values.

Navigating AI in the learning ecosystem is akin to walking on eggshells. Numerous considerations must be taken into account, giving rise to ethical dilemmas. Here are some of the common dilemmas that emerge.

Student Data Privacy

Scenario: Your school adopts an AI-powered learning platform that gathers extensive data on each student's learning behavior, preferences, and performance. The dilemma arises when considering how much of this data is ethically permissible to collect, store, and utilize. Striking a balance between personalized learning benefits and safeguarding student privacy becomes a challenge.

Algorithmic Bias in Grading

Scenario: Your school implements an AI system for grading assignments and tests. The ethical dilemma emerges when you discover that the algorithm exhibits bias, unintentionally favoring or penalizing certain demographics. How do you rectify the biases embedded in the AI grading system to ensure fairness and equal opportunities for all students?

Teacher Autonomy vs. AI Recommendations

Scenario: An AI tool suggests specific teaching strategies or resources to individual teachers based on student data. The ethical question here is whether teachers should unquestioningly follow AI recommendations or retain autonomy in their teaching decisions. Striking a balance between leveraging AI insights and preserving teachers' professional judgment becomes a point of contention.

Equitable Access to AI Resources

Scenario: Your school invests in cutting-edge AI tools to enhance learning experiences. The ethical dilemma arises when it becomes apparent that not all students have equal access to the technology required for these tools. Addressing questions of socioeconomic disparities and ensuring equitable access to AI resources for all students becomes a pressing concern.

AI and Special Education

Scenario: AI is introduced to provide personalized learning experiences, but there needs to be more clarity when it comes to students with special needs. How does AI accommodate diverse learning styles and individualized education plans? Balancing the benefits of AI-driven personalization with the inclusivity required for special education becomes an ethical challenge.

Unveiling the Potential of Biases in AI Algorithms

AI algorithms, essentially sets of rules and instructions for machines to perform tasks, are the backbone of artificial intelligence. However, these algorithms can inadvertently introduce biases, reflecting the data they were trained on and potentially perpetuating unfair or discriminatory outcomes. This phenomenon is known as AI bias. In simple terms, it means that if the data used to train an AI system is biased, the system itself may make biased decisions, leading to unequal treatment of different groups or individuals. This aspect of AI warrants careful examination to ensure fairness and equity in educational settings.

Ultimately, the effectiveness of AI hinges on the information it processes. The outcome is shaped by the data it's fed. This phenomenon occurs when algorithms consistently produce biased results due to flawed assumptions in the machine learning process. In our current environment, characterized by a growing emphasis on representation and diversity, this issue becomes even more critical as algorithms run the risk of perpetuating biases (Larkin, 2022).

As we explore the role of AI in education, it's essential to acknowledge that biases are inherent in our classrooms. These biases manifest in various ways, impacting the learning experience. Consider the following scenarios (Baker & Hawn, 2021).

Gender Biases

Gender biases are unfortunately embedded in AI systems, even in educational tools. For instance, language learning applications powered by AI may inadvertently perpetuate stereotypes related to gender roles and abilities. These apps might recommend distinct vocabulary or present examples based on the gender of the student, contributing to the reinforcement of gender stereotypes. This unintentional bias can hinder the creation of an inclusive and unbiased learning environment, impacting students' perceptions and reinforcing societal norms.

A well-documented example of AI bias related to gender occurred with Amazon's recruiting tool. The company had developed an AI-powered system to assist in the hiring process, but it was later discovered that the tool showed a bias against female candidates. The AI system had been trained on resumes submitted over a ten-year period, and as a result, it learned to prefer resumes that mirrored the predominantly male profiles existing in the dataset.

The biased model penalized resumes that included terms associated with women or women's colleges. Amazon eventually abandoned the tool in 2018 after realizing the unintended gender bias it introduced into the hiring process. This incident highlighted the importance of carefully curating training data to avoid perpetuating societal biases in AI systems (Larkin, 2022).

Racial Bias

Existing AI-powered grading systems may exhibit a tendency to assign lower scores to students from specific racial backgrounds, perpetuating inequalities and affecting fair assessments. For example, an AI grading system might be trained on historical data that reflects systemic biases present in traditional grading practices. If this data contains patterns of racial disparities, the AI model might learn and replicate these biases, leading to unfair evaluations of students belonging to marginalized racial groups.

Many students, particularly those from marginalized racial backgrounds, reported incidents where the software flagged their behavior as suspicious or untrustworthy based on facial recognition algorithms.

In some cases, students with darker skin tones faced difficulties with accurate facial recognition, leading to unjust accusations of cheating or misconduct. This revealed a flaw in the system's design, as it failed to account for diverse facial features and skin tones. The incident shed light on the racial bias embedded in AI technologies, emphasizing the need for thorough testing, evaluation, and adjustments to prevent discriminatory outcomes in educational settings.

Socioeconomic Bias

Socioeconomic bias in AI recommendation systems is a significant concern, influencing the learning experiences of students from different economic backgrounds. These systems, while intended to provide personalized content, can inadvertently reinforce existing educational disparities. For example, a student from a more affluent socioeconomic background might receive recommendations for advanced reading materials and resources, assuming higher proficiency. On the other hand, a student from a less privileged background may be directed toward less challenging content, perpetuating inequalities.

This socioeconomic bias can result in a self-fulfilling prophecy, where students are steered toward materials that align with assumptions about their economic status rather than their actual academic capabilities. The impact of such biases extends beyond the classroom, shaping students' perceptions of their own potential and limiting access to diverse educational opportunities.

To address this issue, it is crucial to scrutinize and refine the algorithms driving these recommendation systems, ensuring they are sensitive to the diversity of socioeconomic backgrounds among students. The goal is to promote equitable access to educational resources and opportunities, fostering an inclusive learning environment that supports the growth and development of all students, regardless of their economic circumstances.

Cultural Bias

Cultural bias in AI-guided history curricula can result in a skewed representation of historical events, emphasizing the contributions of certain cultures while neglecting others. This bias has the potential to limit students' understanding of world history, presenting a one-sided narrative that fails to capture the richness and diversity of global civilizations.

For instance, an AI-driven history curriculum might prioritize the history of dominant cultures, inadvertently marginalizing the contributions and perspectives of historically marginalized or underrepresented communities. Students may miss out on valuable insights into the complex interactions and achievements of diverse cultures throughout history.

Learning Style Bias

Learning style bias can emerge in adaptive learning platforms guided by AI, potentially favoring particular learning styles and disadvantaging students with different preferences, such as auditory or kinesthetic learners. This bias undermines the goal of creating a truly personalized learning experience that accommodates the diverse ways in which students absorb and process information.

For example, an AI-powered adaptive learning system might predominantly cater to visual learners, providing content and assessments that align with this learning style. As a result, auditory learners who thrive through listening or kinesthetic learners who benefit from hands-on activities may not receive content tailored to their strengths.

AI's Impact on Holistic Education in the Standardized Testing Era

It's evident that technological advancements have continuously evolved, shaping the landscape of teaching and learning. From the introduction of the pencil in the 18th century to the emergence of the internet in the 20th, each innovation has played a crucial role in enhancing educational processes.

Today, contemporary classrooms are witnessing the integration of educational technology, ranging from electronic whiteboards to handheld digital devices, providing educators with unprecedented tools to optimize the learning experiences of their students. Among these technologies, AI stands out as a potent force, demonstrating remarkable effectiveness in facilitating personalized and individualized instruction (Smith, 2022).

As we appreciate the role of AI in education, it's essential to explore the potential unintended consequences, one of which involves the inadvertent emphasis on standardized test results over a holistic approach to education. While AI has demonstrated its ability to personalize instruction, there is a risk that, in the pursuit of measurable outcomes, the emphasis on standardized testing might overshadow the broader goal of nurturing well-rounded, critical-thinking individuals.

It is true that an AI-driven adaptive learning system aiming to boost test scores focuses predominantly on drilling students with test-specific content. While this may result in improved exam performance, it also risks overshadowing broader educational goals.

Consider Jade, a high school student with a passion for creative writing. The AI, designed to prioritize standardized test preparation, guides her toward exercises solely aligned with test formats. In this pursuit of elevated test scores, the system inadvertently neglects Jade's unique talents and stifles her creative potential. The unintended consequence is a narrowed educational experience that favors test-centric proficiency over holistic skill development.

Moreover, teachers find themselves navigating the delicate balance between adhering to standardized testing requirements and fostering a well-rounded education. The pressure to meet stringent performance metrics may inadvertently lead educators to prioritize teaching methods solely geared toward exam success. The result is a potential loss of emphasis on critical thinking, problem-solving, and creativity—pillars of a holistic education.

This inadvertent shift not only affects individual students but also permeates the entire educational culture. Schools, driven by the need to showcase strong test results, may allocate resources disproportionately to test-centric strategies, leaving behind a void in the development of essential life skills.

The implications are profound, urging us to reflect on whether our current AI-driven educational landscape strikes the right balance between preparing students for standardized tests and nurturing their broader capabilities. As we navigate this terrain, it becomes imperative to reevaluate the role of AI in education, ensuring that it serves as a tool that enhances, rather than hinders, the holistic development of students.

The Risk of Over-Reliance on Technology

Imagine a future in education where the surge in technology adoption reaches a point where the very essence of teaching and the unique human touch is at risk of fading away. As educators, we've witnessed the integration of virtual classes, AI-driven knowledge delivery, and automated systems into our classrooms. While these advancements offer undeniable benefits, there's a potential downside: the risk of sidelining the vital human element in our profession.

Consider the implications for our classrooms and lecture halls. The dynamic interactions between us and our students, those "aha" moments of shared discovery, and the mentorship that extends beyond the curriculum could be diluted in an environment dominated by screens and algorithms.

Now, think back to the impactful teachers in your life—the ones who not only shared knowledge but also inspired, motivated, and helped shape your journey. Picture a scenario where those profound interactions are overshadowed by the hum of machines and the impersonal nature of virtual learning.

The risk we face isn't just about the transformation of education; it's about preserving the very skills and qualities that make us effective educators. The fusion of technology and the human touch is where the magic happens, but an overreliance on the former threatens to upset this delicate balance.

Strategies for Ensuring Data Privacy

In our ever-evolving educational landscape, one of the paramount ethical challenges we face is the potential breach of student data privacy due to the integration of AI.

In a Nordic saga of privacy missteps, a school district in Skellefteå, Sweden, found itself in a legal quandary. The unnamed high school, on an experimental quest, employed a facial recognition and artificial intelligence system to monitor student attendance from September to December of 2019. However, their journey took an unfortunate turn when the European Data Protection Board imposed a fine of 200,000 Swedish Krona (approximately $20,700) upon the municipality overseeing the school. The violation was rooted in breaching privacy and biometrics provisions laid out in the General Data Protection Regulation (GDPR).

The school's facial recognition foray, designed to streamline attendance tracking, unraveled as an unlawful processing of sensitive biometric data, as per GDPR guidelines. Adding to the transgressions, the municipality failed to duly inform Sweden's Data Protection Authority about its pilot program, a procedural lapse under GDPR.

Despite claims of initiating the pilot program with student consent, the Swedish Data Protection Authority countered that the consent lacked legal validity due to a stark imbalance between the pupils (data subjects) and the municipality (data controller). The repercussions were swift, with a GDPR stipulated fine that could have amounted to €1 million, highlighting the gravity of GDPR compliance.

This cautionary tale underscores the growing global concern around facial recognition and AI technologies, emphasizing the need for strict adherence to privacy regulations. In a world grappling with identity theft, data misuse, and unauthorized tracking, GDPR serves as a guardian, demanding meticulous procedures to protect sensitive information (Asokan, 2019).

As the stewards of student information, it is our responsibility to proactively secure this sensitive data and maintain the trust bestowed upon us by students, parents, and the wider educational community.

General Data Protection Regulation (GDPR)

In our commitment to safeguarding student data, it's crucial to be well-versed in the GDPR or local data protection regulations applicable in your region. GDPR serves as a comprehensive framework designed to protect individuals' privacy rights, and it plays a pivotal role in shaping how we handle student data.

GDPR provides a set of guidelines and regulations on how personal data, including that of students, should be collected, processed, and stored. It empowers individuals with greater control over their information, ensuring transparency and accountability in data handling practices.

Steps to navigate GDPR (Llywodraeth et al. Government, 2020):

- Ensure that your school's leadership, including the headteacher and senior leadership team, comprehensively understands how GDPR applies to learner and staff data. Utilize online resources, especially those provided by the Information Commissioner's Office (ICO), to take the initial steps toward compliance.
- As a school processing personal data, it is mandatory to register with the ICO as a data controller, aligning with GDPR requirements.
- Take stock of the data your school processes by conducting a comprehensive data audit. This understanding allows you to secure data safely and ensure appropriate storage.
- In compliance with GDPR, appoint a data protection officer to delve into the complexities of this new requirement.

- Review consent practices, ensuring they align with GDPR's definition of a "freely given, specific, informed, and unambiguous indication of the individual's wishes." Be aware that consent is just one of six legal bases for processing data.
- Provide data protection training to all staff, tailoring it to the specific data they handle daily. Regular training ensures everyone understands their obligations.
- Regularly review your school's data protection policy, a foundational document that guides staff on their obligations and practices. Ensure all staff members are trained on and have read the policy.
- Involve school governors as a valuable source of support and expertise. Given their role in the senior leadership team, they also share responsibility for school data.
- Develop and test comprehensive incident management and recovery plans to swiftly recover from data loss or cyber-attacks. These plans also play a preventive role, minimizing the likelihood of such incidents.
- Leverage available GDPR guidance, particularly from the ICO's website. For additional support, consider local authorities. Should specialized support be required, conduct due diligence on the experience and knowledge of legal or consulting services before engaging them.

By proactively addressing these steps, schools can strengthen their GDPR compliance, ensuring robust data protection measures.

The Imperative of Regularly Reviewing Terms of Service

It is paramount to underscore the importance of routinely reviewing and updating terms of service with AI vendors as we integrate AI deeper into the strands of education. Much like the broader technological sphere, algorithms, and AI tools necessitate continuous scrutiny to pinpoint any potential disparate impact on users, particularly in relation to protected categories defined by federal and state laws (The Legal Intelligencer, 2023).

As educational institutions embrace AI technologies to enhance learning experiences, the responsibility lies not only in the initial selection of AI tools but also in an ongoing commitment to monitoring their impact. This vigilance ensures that the adoption of AI aligns with the principles of fairness, equity, and compliance with legal regulations.

Regular reviews of terms of service serve as a proactive measure to identify and rectify any unintended consequences or biases that may emerge over time. By engaging in this practice, educators can contribute to fostering an AI-in-education ecosystem that upholds ethical standards, prioritizes inclusivity, and provides an equitable learning environment for all students.

Using Anonymized Student Data

Anonymizing student data stands as a linchpin in the fortress of student privacy. This strategic approach involves meticulously removing any personal identifiers intricately linked to an individual student, rendering the data anonymous. Picture it as a protective cloak, shielding sensitive information from prying eyes while still allowing educators and AI systems to derive valuable insights.

Consider a scenario where AI algorithms analyze anonymized test scores across a school district. Without compromising privacy, educators can gain valuable insights into overall academic performance trends, identify areas for improvement, and tailor instructional strategies. It's akin to peering into a collective academic journey without singling out individual students.

This anonymization process is not just a safeguard—it is an enabler. It enables the utilization of vast datasets for educational research, curriculum development, and the enhancement of teaching methodologies without compromising the individual privacy of students. It strikes a delicate balance, fostering a climate of trust and progress within the educational landscape.

To fortify this commitment to privacy, educators can adopt the five principles that form a robust shield around student data:

1. **Transparency:** Keep a clear line of communication open. Ensure that students, parents, and educators are aware of the

types of data being collected, how they will be used, and the purpose they serve in enhancing education.
2. **No commercial uses:** Student data should be treated with the utmost care and should not be exploited for commercial gains. It is essential to establish a boundary that prevents the use of this data for marketing or other noneducational purposes.
3. **Security protections:** Implement robust security measures to safeguard student data. Encryption, secure networks, and access controls are vital components of a comprehensive security strategy.
4. **Parental and student rights:** Afford parents and students the right to control and access their own data. This empowers them to make informed decisions about the use of their information.
5. **Enforcement:** Establish and enforce policies that prioritize the protection of student data. This includes holding both educational institutions and technology providers accountable for any breaches or misuse.

AI Tool Ethical Consideration Checklist for Educators

Before incorporating a new AI tool into your educational repertoire, it is essential to critically evaluate its ethical implications. Use the checklist below to ensure that the AI tool aligns with ethical standards and promotes a positive learning environment.

Student Data Privacy

- Does the AI tool adhere to data protection regulations, such as GDPR?
- Is student data anonymized and securely stored?
- Does the tool have a clear data usage policy?

Bias and Fairness

- Has the AI tool been tested for biases in its algorithms?
- Can the tool's decisions be explained transparently?
- Does it account for and mitigate biases related to gender, race, and socioeconomic factors?

Informed Consent

- Is there a transparent process for obtaining informed consent from students and parents?
- Do users fully understand how their data will be used by the AI tool?

Accessibility

- Is the AI tool designed to accommodate students with diverse learning needs?
- Does it provide equal opportunities for students with disabilities?

Educational Impact

- Will the AI tool enhance the overall learning experience?
- Does it support personalized learning without compromising the human touch in teaching?

Security

- How secure is the AI tool against potential cyber threats?
- Is there a plan for managing and mitigating security breaches?

Parental Involvement

- Is there a mechanism for keeping parents informed about the AI tool's use?
- Can parents provide input or raise concerns about the tool's impact on their children?

Long-Term Effects

- Has the AI tool undergone a thorough assessment of its long-term impact on students' development?

- Are there plans for ongoing evaluations and adjustments based on feedback?

Ethical Framework

- Does the AI tool align with the ethical guidelines and values of the educational institution?
- Can the tool be integrated within the existing ethical framework of the school?

Professional Development

- Are educators provided with adequate training on using and overseeing the AI tool?
- Is ongoing professional development offered to ensure educators stay informed about the tool's evolving features?

Using this checklist can empower you to make informed decisions about the ethical implications of AI tools, fostering a responsible and positive technological environment in education.

In this chapter, we delved into the complex ethical considerations surrounding AI in education. We dissected potential biases and highlighted the importance of safeguarding student data privacy. The journey revealed that while AI promises transformative benefits, its implementation requires careful ethical navigation.

As we unravel the layers of ethics surrounding AI, it's clear that technology's role in the classroom is not just black or white. Let's explore how AI is not just about algorithms and data. It's about individualized learning experiences, ensuring every student gets a tailor-made education suited just for them. Welcome to the world of personalized learning powered by AI.

3

TAILOR-MADE TEACHING—AI'S ROLE IN PERSONALIZED LEARNING

Did you know that in the ever-evolving landscape of education, half of educators describe personalized learning as not just a buzzword but a powerful tool in the school improvement toolbox? A survey by the Education Week Research Center uncovered this insight, revealing the promise that personalized learning holds (Kurtz et al., 2018).

Personalized learning isn't just a pedagogical trend; it's a dynamic approach to education that acknowledges the diversity of learners. Imagine a classroom where each student's journey is curated based on their strengths, learning style, and pace. That's the essence of personalized learning.

The Mechanics of Personalized AI-Driven Learning

Think of it as a customized journey, a teaching approach that acknowledges the individuality of each learner. It's about recognizing that every learner has a distinct learning style, pace, and set of strengths and weaknesses. AI acts as the compass guiding this personalized educational journey. But how does it work its magic?

Understanding Learning Patterns

AI begins by meticulously observing and analyzing students' learning patterns. Every interaction, every response to an exercise, and every moment spent on a lesson provides valuable data.

Data, the Fuel for Customization

This data becomes the fuel for AI's customization engine. The more it knows about a student, the better it becomes at predicting their needs and optimizing their learning experience.

Adapting Content in Real Time

Imagine a scenario where Alexa, a student, excels in mathematical problem-solving but struggles with algebraic concepts. AI recognizes this pattern and, in real-time, adjusts the content to offer more challenging problems in problem-solving while providing additional support in algebra.

Mastery-Based Progression

Here's the beauty of it: AI doesn't adhere to a fixed timeline. It allows students to progress at their own pace, ensuring mastery before moving forward. No rushing through lessons, no being held back by a predefined schedule.

Continuous Feedback Loop

As students engage, AI provides instant feedback. This isn't just about grading; it's about offering insights into strengths and areas for improvement. The feedback loop is a continuous process, shaping the learning journey dynamically.

Adaptive Assessments

Traditional exams can be daunting, especially when they don't consider individual strengths and weaknesses. AI-driven assessments adapt, presenting questions that align with a student's proficiency level, ensuring a fair evaluation.

Personalization Beyond Subjects

It's not just about math or literature. AI extends its personalization prowess to extracurriculars, suggesting reading materials, projects, or activities aligned with a student's interests and aspirations.

The result is a harmonious educational experience where learning isn't just imparted but deeply absorbed. The magic is in the details, and AI is here to help you orchestrate an educational masterpiece.

Every student in your class has a distinctive way of learning. Some are visual learners, and others thrive on hands-on activities. As you recommend a mix of resources like videos, interactive simulations, articles, and practical projects, you're ensuring that each student engages with the content in a way that clicks for them. It's about providing a personalized learning journey.

In your classroom, students span a range of proficiency levels. By suggesting materials with different complexity levels, you're addressing this diversity. Advanced learners get the challenge they seek, while those needing extra support access materials designed for foundational understanding.

Education shouldn't be static. Keep your students informed about the latest developments by recommending current articles, podcasts, or documentaries related to your subjects. It's about instilling a sense of curiosity and showing them the dynamic nature of knowledge.

Revolutionizing Assessments: AI's Adaptive Quiz and Assignment Evolution

Picture this: a student faces a quiz, and AI is at work behind the scenes. As they navigate through questions, the system adapts to the difficulty based on their performance. It's not a generic test; it's a personalized challenge that precisely measures their abilities. The result? A more accurate reflection of what each student truly knows.

The evolution of AI in the education ecosystem says one thing: No more stacks of papers for you! AI ensures a swift and accurate grading process, relieving educators of the tedious aspects of assessment. Moreover, it brings an added benefit for students—prompt feedback. This not only reduces their anxiety about waiting for grades but also contributes to a smoother and more interactive learning journey. The evolution of education with AI is marking a shift toward efficiency and enhanced student engagement.

AI is leading us into a world where grading is fair, consistent, and entirely unbiased. AI is an objective scorer. The beauty lies in its ability to maintain a standardized evaluation process, free from the influence of human bias.

Picture this scenario: A stack of essays or open-ended responses, each showcasing a student's unique perspective. Now, instead of relying on the subjective judgment of an individual, AI algorithms take charge. They analyze the content based on predefined criteria, ensuring that every answer is measured against the same standard.

No longer do personal preferences, unconscious biases, or fatigue influence the grading process. AI's objectivity ensures that each student's work is evaluated fairly, providing an equal opportunity for everyone. It's not just a wishful thought; it's a tangible step toward a more equitable educational landscape.

AI is now employed to evaluate the performance of students engaged in group projects and collaborative learning settings. By scrutinizing data, including student interactions, contributions, and communication patterns, AI offers valuable insights into each student's role within the group and their individual achievements. This data proves instrumental for you in pinpointing students who might be encountering challenges or not actively participating in the group (Frąckiewicz, 2023b)

Now, think of AI as your data wizard. It doesn't just collect assessment information; it unveils patterns and trends. Imagine having insights into your student's learning behaviors and performance trends. This data-driven approach empowers you to make informed decisions about your teaching strategies, tailoring your instruction to address specific needs.

AI Predictive Abilities

AI opens up exciting possibilities for educators to proactively support students in areas where they may face challenges. By harnessing the power of data and advanced algorithms, AI has the remarkable ability to predict potential struggle points and offer invaluable insights into individual student learning journeys. Imagine having a tool that not only identifies areas of difficulty but also crafts tailored interventions, creating a learning environment that is responsive and personalized.

- **Creating tailored learning materials:** AI analyzes a student's learning patterns, strengths, and weaknesses, and then, like an expert tailor, it stitches together customized learning materials. Whether it's adapting the complexity of text, adjusting the pace of exercises, or incorporating multimedia elements, AI ensures that each student receives content designed specifically for their learning journey.
- **Providing multiple ways to present information:** AI understands that students have diverse preferences for grasping concepts. Some might thrive through visual aids, while others prefer textual explanations. AI, acting as a versatile guide, tailors its methods, ensuring that information is not only presented but presented in a way that resonates with each student's unique learning style.
- **Designing alternative and authentic assessments:** AI shakes up the traditional assessment scene. No more monotonous exams that only scratch the surface of understanding. Instead, AI suggests alternative and authentic assessments. Picture this: students showcase their comprehension not through standardized tests but through projects, presentations, or practical applications. AI recognizes that this multifaceted evaluation not only captures the depth of understanding but also nurtures creativity and critical thinking.
- **Breaking down complex skills:** AI recognizes that students aren't just vessels to fill with information but individuals with unique strengths and styles of learning. It paves the way for personalized, comprehensive evaluations by suggesting alternative and authentic assessments.

Real-World Applications

AI has emerged as a transformative force, reshaping traditional paradigms and ushering in an era of personalized learning experiences.

Various AI tools have played pivotal roles in tailoring education to individual needs, providing educators and students with innovative solutions that transcend conventional boundaries. These game-changers have not only streamlined administrative tasks but have also significantly enhanced the quality and accessibility of educational content (Eklavvya Assessments, 2023).

AI Question Paper Generator

Creating exam papers can be a real challenge, right? The AI Question Paper Generator is here to save the day. Just feed it your content, specify your question preferences, and *voilà*! It crafts a tailored question paper based on difficulty, age group, and skills to be assessed. This wizardry tool generates a paper that meets your needs.

Carnegie Learning

Struggling with helping students grasp math concepts? Carnegie Learning brings AI-powered math education to your classroom. Using machine learning, it delivers interactive lessons and real-time feedback. Whether you're tackling algebra or calculus, this tool's got your back.

Eklavvya AI Proctoring

This is a great tool if you are worried about maintaining exam integrity during online assessments. This web-based system keeps an eye on students during exams, using AI to analyze facial expressions and behavior. It's the guardian of online assessments, ensuring they're secure and malpractice-free.

Smart Sparrow

If you are looking for an adaptive e-learning platform, Smart Sparrow's got your back. Using AI tailors learning experiences, providing real-time feedback. No more one-size-fits-all lessons; it's personalized learning at its finest.

DreamBox

DreamBox, an adaptive K-8 math education platform, uses AI to personalize learning experiences. It adjusts lesson difficulty on the fly, offering real-time feedback.

Nearpod

This learning platform goes beyond the ordinary by integrating AI to craft captivating and immersive lessons. With a rich library of ready-to-use content and the flexibility for educators to customize presentations, quizzes, and virtual reality experiences, Nearpod transforms learning into an engaging adventure.

Squirrel AI Learning

This AI-driven marvel assesses individual strengths and weaknesses using machine learning algorithms. The outcome? Customized lessons and real-time feedback that guide each student on an optimized learning journey. Squirrel AI combines the best of human tutoring with the precision of AI.

Thinkster Math

This app seamlessly blends human tutors with AI technology to deliver personalized instruction and practice. Tailored math programs address specific needs, enhancing problem-solving skills and mathematical proficiency for a top-notch learning experience.

Quizlet

As a teacher, you're always tweaking your methods for the best outcomes. Quizlet, a study and learning platform, uses AI to create dynamic flashcards, quizzes, and study games. The AI algorithms adapt to individual learning patterns, optimizing study sessions and offering personalized recommendations to boost retention across various subjects. It's like having a personalized learning assistant at your fingertips!

Writely AI

Harnessing the power of natural language processing and machine learning algorithms, Writely AI provides real-time suggestions to enhance grammar, style, and clarity. It goes beyond traditional feedback, pinpointing areas for improvement and suggesting alternative wording. By incorporating Writely AI, students can elevate their writing skills, foster stronger communication abilities, and ultimately improve academic performance.

Google Bard

This AI-powered tool focuses on the art of generating poetry and creative written content. Using natural language processing and deep learning algorithms, Google Bard can craft original poems, rhymes, and verses across a broad spectrum of topics. Engage your students with Bard for an uninterrupted interactive learning experience available 24/7. With its knack for understanding context, structure, and wordplay, Google Bard has become a wellspring of inspiration in language arts education. Teachers can seamlessly integrate Google Bard into their curriculum to spark creativity, introduce poetic techniques, and nurture students' unique writing voices.

ChatGPT

This versatile AI tool has left its mark across diverse domains, with education being no exception. In the realm of education, ChatGPT emerges as a natural language-based AI companion, providing dynamic responses to your queries. Its learning capabilities and natural language processing prowess extend a helping hand to educators, simplifying the creation of high-quality study notes. But that's not all—ChatGPT goes beyond by serving as a reliable teaching assistant for your students.

Kaltura

Kaltura's AI-powered video platform brings innovation to education, encompassing a video management system, a video creation platform, and a video collaboration tool. Educators can seamlessly create, manage, and share video content, enhancing the learning experience through dynamic multimedia engagement.

Edmentum

Experience personalized learning like never before with Edmentum, an AI-powered platform designed to tailor educational experiences for students. Edmentum employs machine learning algorithms to assess individual strengths and weaknesses, offering targeted instruction and real-time feedback. Through this dynamic approach, students can strive toward their full potential with a customized learning path.

Edmodo

Edmodo goes beyond traditional communication and collaboration tools by employing AI to personalize learning experiences. Real-time feedback and insights into student performance further contribute to an enriched learning process, fostering a connected and dynamic educational community.

The landscape is rich with diverse tools, each bringing its unique strengths to the forefront. The onus lies with you to embark on a journey of exploration and research, scouting the vast array of options to find the tools that resonate most with your teaching philosophies and the individual needs of your students. This dynamic and expansive field ensures that there's a fitting solution for every educational context, encouraging you to be proactive in discovering the tools that will bring about the desired outcomes in your students' overall learning experiences.

AI in Education: Reflect, Predict, and Collaborate

AI Impact Reflection

1. Reflect on how AI has already influenced your teaching methods and classroom dynamics.
2. Consider the positive aspects and any challenges you may have encountered.
3. Note down specific examples of AI tools you've found effective or areas where improvement is needed.

Personalized Learning Assessment

- Evaluate the effectiveness of personalized learning in your classroom.
- Identify AI tools that have contributed to personalized learning experiences.
- Assess the impact on student engagement, understanding, and overall academic performance.

Future Predictions

- Given your understanding of AI's current role in education, predict its evolution in the next five or ten years.
- Envision how AI might enhance or change teaching methods, student interactions, and the overall learning experience.
- Consider potential challenges and benefits, fostering a forward-thinking mindset.

AI-Enhanced Lesson Plan

- Design a lesson plan that incorporates AI tools to enhance the learning experience.
- Specify how AI will be integrated, what aspects it will address, and the expected outcomes.
- Reflect on how this approach aligns with your educational objectives and benefits students.

Student Feedback Session

- Engage students in a discussion about their experiences with AI tools in the classroom.
- Gather feedback on what worked well, what could be improved, and their overall comfort with AI integration.
- Use their insights to adapt and refine your approach to AI in education.

Continuous Learning Plan

- Develop a plan for your continuous learning in the field of AI and education.
- Identify resources, courses, or communities that can keep you updated on the latest AI advancements.
- Consider how staying informed aligns with your commitment to providing quality education.

Student-Centric AI Implementation

- Brainstorm ways to involve students in the integration of AI tools in the learning process.
- Consider seeking their input on tool selection, providing feedback, and adjusting AI-enhanced activities based on their preferences.

AI in Parental Engagement

- Explore how AI can be used to enhance communication with parents about student progress.
- Consider AI-driven platforms that offer insights into individual student achievements and areas for improvement.
- Reflect on the potential benefits and challenges of involving parents in the AI-enhanced educational journey.

As you've seen, AI's transformative power doesn't stop at personalizing lessons. Its influence extends to sparking a keen interest and heightened involvement from students. Are you ready to witness how AI can make classes more interactive, engaging, and downright irresistible for students? Dive into the next chapter as we explore the exhilarating world of AI-driven student engagement.

4

ENGAGING MINDS—AI'S ROLE IN ELEVATING STUDENT ENGAGEMENT

> *"The function of education is to teach one to think intensively and to think critically. Intelligence plus character—that is the goal of true education."*
> –Martin Luther King, Jr

As we dive into this chapter, we are not just exploring technology for technology's sake. We're talking about real, practical ways artificial intelligence can make a tangible impact on student engagement in your classroom. Whether you are a seasoned educator or just starting your teaching journey, understanding these AI-driven engagement strategies can be a game-changer.

AI-Driven Tools and Strategies for Engagement

Adaptive Learning Platforms

Adaptive learning platforms are like the personal tutors of the digital age. These AI-driven systems analyze individual students' progress, learning styles, and performance data. As students interact with the platform, it adapts, tweaking the content to suit each student's strengths and weaknesses. Imagine a system that knows exactly when to speed up, slow down, or delve deeper into a topic based on a student's responses. It's personalized learning on steroids. This adaptability not only caters to diverse learning needs but also keeps students challenged at their optimal learning pace, preventing boredom or overwhelm.

Gamified Learning Apps

Gamified learning apps bring an element of play into education. They leverage game mechanics to make learning fun and engaging. Points, rewards, and competition turn mundane tasks into exciting challenges. These apps often incorporate interactive quizzes, quests, and challenges that students can conquer to earn rewards or move up levels. The competitive edge taps into the natural desire for achievement, creating a sense of accomplishment that keeps students motivated. The result? Learning becomes a thrilling adventure rather than a chore.

Virtual Reality Setups

Virtual reality (VR) takes education to a whole new dimension—literally. Imagine students not just reading about historical events but actually "being" there or exploring the intricacies of the solar system by "traveling" through it. VR setups provide immersive experiences that traditional methods can't match. The visual and interactive elements stimulate multiple senses, enhancing retention and understanding. Students are no longer passive observers; they are active participants in their learning journey. The wow factor of VR not only captures attention but also fosters a deeper connection with the subject matter.

In a nutshell, these AI-driven tools revolutionize engagement by tailoring learning experiences, infusing excitement into lessons, and transporting students to new realms of understanding. The classroom becomes a place of dynamic interaction, where education is not just absorbed but experienced.

Strategies for Engagement

To go the extra mile in ensuring student engagement, you ought to put the following strategies into play:

- **Interactive assessments:** Shift from traditional assessments to interactive ones. Instead of standard quizzes, use platforms that offer adaptive questioning based on individual performance. For instance, tools like Quizizz allow students to answer at their own pace, making the learning experience more dynamic.
- **Collaborative projects:** Foster collaboration by assigning projects that encourage teamwork. Tools like Google Workspace provide real-time collaboration, enabling students to work collectively on documents, presentations, or spreadsheets. This not only enhances engagement but also develops crucial teamwork and communication skills.
- **Discussion forums:** Create an online space for discussions. Platforms like Padlet or Flipgrid allow students to share thoughts, opinions, or multimedia content. This promotes active participation, ensuring that even quieter students have a voice. Engaging discussions extend beyond the classroom, providing a continuous learning environment.
- **Real-world applications:** Connect lessons to real-world applications. For instance, in a physics class, instead of just teaching about velocity, introduce a project where students analyze real car crash data. This application of knowledge sparks interest and demonstrates the practical relevance of what they are learning.
- **Feedback mechanisms:** Implement instant feedback mechanisms. Tools like Kahoot! provide immediate feedback

during quizzes. This not only keeps students informed about their performance but also turns assessment into a gamified experience, making the learning process more enjoyable.
- **Personalized learning paths:** Embrace platforms that offer personalized learning paths. For example, tools like Khan Academy adapt content based on individual progress. This ensures that each student learns at their own pace, preventing boredom or frustration often associated with one-size-fits-all approaches.
- **Incorporate multimedia:** Integrate multimedia elements into lessons. Platforms like Nearpod allow you to create interactive lessons with videos, simulations, or virtual field trips. Visual and auditory stimuli enhance engagement, catering to various learning preferences.
- **Guest speakers or virtual tours:** Bring the outside world into the classroom. Arrange virtual sessions with guest speakers or organize virtual tours using platforms like Zoom or Microsoft Teams. This exposes students to diverse perspectives and experiences, making learning more vibrant.
- **Choice-based learning:** Offer choices in assignments. Platforms like SymbalooEDU allow you to curate a selection of resources, letting students choose how they want to explore a topic. Autonomy in learning fosters a sense of ownership and enthusiasm.

Application Reflection

In the space below, share one innovative idea or strategy inspired by the AI-driven engagement tools discussed. How can you envision implementing it in your classroom to enhance student engagement?

The Power of Chatbots

Chatbots are computer programs designed to simulate conversations with human users, especially over the Internet. These AI applications are equipped with natural language processing capabilities, allowing them to understand and respond to user queries and prompts. Chatbots can be implemented on various platforms, such as websites, messaging applications, or virtual assistants, to provide instant and automated interaction, answer questions, offer information, or assist with tasks in a conversational manner. They play a significant role in enhancing the user experience, automating customer support, and facilitating efficient communication in diverse contexts.

Let's unravel the ways in which chatbots and AI-driven content recommendations can become invaluable allies in supporting student learning. As an educator, you ought to embrace a dynamic classroom where these tools contribute not only to academic assistance but also to cultivating a proactive learning environment.

Chatbots come in as virtual assistants available 24/7 to assist students with their homework. Chatbots step in as reliable companions, offering real-time feedback and personalized suggestions for further study. As educators, you can extend the use of chatbots beyond the traditional classroom setting. Picture them as an additional support system for your students, providing instant clarification and guidance whenever they need it.

The utilization of AI, like ChatGPT, is not just accepted but encouraged as a supplementary reference tool. This inclusion sets the stage for an open and innovative approach to learning, fostering an environment where students can leverage AI responsibly.

Consider using AI as a reference guide to elucidate complex topics. As an educator, you can demonstrate to your students how AI can serve as an additional resource for clarifying concepts. This encourages an interactive learning approach where technology becomes a seamless part of the learning journey, aiding students in comprehending challenging subjects more effectively.

Encourage your students to explore AI tools independently. They can use these tools outside of class to gain further insights into concepts that might be causing confusion. By doing so, students take charge of their learning experience, utilizing AI as a study companion that supports and augments their understanding.

Engage your students in discussions about the practical applications of AI in their future career fields. Highlight how AI is not just a classroom tool but a skill set that will be increasingly relevant in various professions. Encouraging students to explore AI's future applications empowers them to be proactive in adapting to evolving technological landscapes.

In essence, the integration of chatbots and AI-driven content recommendations is not just about answering homework questions; it's about fostering a culture of curiosity and independent exploration. As educators, you have the opportunity to guide your students in responsibly navigating the landscape of AI, ensuring it becomes a valuable asset in their academic journey and beyond (Centre for Teaching Excellence, n.d.).

Revolutionizing History Education: The Impact of Virtual Reality Technologies on Student Engagement

In the realm of education, the integration of cutting-edge technologies has become a transformative force. A noteworthy example is the incorporation of VR environments into history education, sparking considerable interest among students.

A case study, which employed a sampling of 25 undergraduate students, delved into their perspectives on virtual reality technologies, specifically focusing on the use of VR glasses in history education. The findings revealed a unanimous appreciation for virtual reality implementations among the participants.

The students expressed that integrating such immersive technology into their coursework not only enhanced their learning experience but also had a positive impact on their engagement levels. Notably, the sense of reality and the feeling of being present in historical locations, facilitated by virtual reality, emerged as pivotal factors influencing the students and kindling a heightened interest in the subject matter.

Beyond mere enthusiasm, the study suggested that virtual reality technologies could potentially address accessibility challenges, providing a means for individuals with disabilities or various limitations (financial, time constraints, etc.) to actively participate in the learning process. The results underscored the belief that embracing current technology in educational activities could bring about substantial benefits, fostering a more inclusive and engaging learning environment (Gürkan et al., 2018).

Measuring the Success of AI Tools

Measuring the success of AI tools is only possible through engaging the students, and this can be enhanced through a feedback loop mechanism. Feedback stands as a cornerstone, acting as the compass guiding students on their learning journey. It's not just about correcting errors; feedback is the beacon that illuminates the path toward improvement.

But what exactly is feedback, and why is it so vital in the context of personalized learning enhanced by AI tools? Feedback, in its essence, is a dynamic communication loop that encompasses various forms of information about one's performance.

One of the hallmarks of AI-driven education lies in its ability to offer real-time feedback to students. Imagine a learning environment where the moment a student tackles a challenge, the system responds instantly, providing insights into their performance. AI content tools precisely achieve this feat by offering immediate feedback on a student's actions and responses. This instantaneous response mechanism empowers students in a unique way—the ability to learn from their mistakes on the spot. It's a dynamic process where errors are not just corrected but transformed into valuable learning opportunities.

Beyond the immediate correction, the significance of feedback in personalized learning extends to broader dimensions. Feedback acts as a vigilant companion, helping students monitor their progress systematically. Instead of waiting for periodic assessments, students receive continuous updates on their performance, creating a proactive approach to their learning journey.

Furthermore, feedback proves to be a potent motivator. The acknowledgment of accomplishments, no matter how small, fuels a sense of achievement and encourages students to persist in their academic pursuits. This motivational boost, intertwined with constructive criticism, shapes a positive learning environment where challenges are viewed as stepping stones to improvement.

Feedback serves as a guiding light for instructors. It provides crucial insights that inform instructional strategies. Understanding how students engage with the material allows educators to tailor their approach, ensuring it resonates with the unique needs of each learner.

Moreover, feedback becomes a catalyst for self-reflection and goal-setting. Students, armed with insights into their strengths and areas for improvement, can actively reflect on their learning journey. This reflective process sets the stage for setting realistic goals, transforming the educational experience into a dynamic, evolving partnership between the learner and the knowledge at hand.

Leveraging AI Analytics for Enhanced Student Engagement

AI analytics involves the systematic analysis of data generated by AI tools and systems to extract meaningful insights. In the educational context, this encompasses a spectrum of data points, ranging from student interactions with learning platforms to performance metrics on assessments. Essentially, AI analytics transforms raw data into actionable intelligence, providing educators with a nuanced understanding of student behavior, participation, and progress.

Examples of AI Analytics in Education

Here are a few examples of AI analytics effectiveness in the education ecosystem:

1. **Participation metrics:** AI analytics can track students' active involvement in online discussions, group projects, or interactive learning modules. It quantifies participation levels, shedding light on collaborative efforts and individual contributions.
2. **Time-on-task analysis:** By monitoring the time students spend on specific tasks or assignments, AI analytics unveils insights into their engagement levels. Understanding where students invest their time can guide you in refining instructional strategies.
3. **Scoring and improvement patterns:** AI analytics can assess students' performance data over time, highlighting trends and patterns. You gain visibility into areas of improvement, allowing for targeted interventions to enhance learning outcomes (Ouyang et al., 2023).

Utilizing AI Analytics for Enhanced Student Engagement

We have acknowledged how crucial AI analytics are as far as student engagement is concerned. Here is a breakdown of how this can be achieved:

Customizing Learning Paths

- Insight: AI analytics can identify individual learning preferences and areas of struggle.
- Application: You can tailor learning paths, recommending content and activities that align with each student's learning style and addressing specific challenges.

Real-time Intervention

- Insight: Immediate identification of students falling behind or disengaging.
- Application: Educators can promptly intervene with personalized support, whether through additional resources, one-on-one sessions, or targeted feedback.

Adaptive Assessments

- Insight: Continuous evaluation of student performance.
- Application: AI analytics inform the creation of adaptive assessments, adjusting difficulty levels based on individual progress and ensuring a challenging yet manageable learning experience.

Feedback Loop Enhancement

- Insight: Understanding how students respond to feedback.
- Application: Educators can refine feedback strategies, aligning them with student preferences and optimizing the feedback loop for maximum impact on engagement and improvement.

Identifying Engagement Patterns

- Insight: Recognizing when students are most and least engaged.
- Application: Time-sensitive adjustments can be made to lesson plans, ensuring peak engagement during high-impact periods.

Application Reflection

In the space below, share one innovative idea or strategy inspired by the AI-driven engagement tools discussed. How can you envision implementing it in your classroom to enhance student engagement?

Decoding Observational Data in the Classroom

As dedicated educators, we understand the pivotal role student engagement plays in shaping not only academic success but also laying the foundation for future accomplishments. In our pursuit of cultivating vibrant and participative classrooms, it becomes imperative to unravel the dynamics of student behavior, involvement, and enthusiasm.

Our observations underscore a noteworthy correlation between students' performance (SP) and the messages crafted by teachers. It appears that the better the students perform, the higher the likelihood of encountering engaging messages. As educators, this insight serves as a compass, guiding us to tailor our communication in a manner that resonates with students, fostering not only understanding but also a genuine enthusiasm for learning (Falcon et al., 2023).

Based on a study conducted by Falcon and colleagues (2023), we unearthed a relationship between students' performance and the use of extrinsic messages. It seems that as students excel, their inclination toward employing extrinsic motivational messages increases. Recognizing this, we are prompted to explore diverse and personalized ways of inspiring our students, acknowledging that motivations can be as varied as the learners themselves.

An intriguing revelation surfaces when we consider teachers' enthusiasm for teaching (ET) in the equation. It appears that the passion and energy we bring into our teaching domain are intricately linked to the nature of the engaging messages we deliver. As we infuse our lessons with enthusiasm, the likelihood of crafting messages that captivate and inspire our students amplifies. This emphasizes the profound impact our own passion can have on fostering a dynamic and engaging learning environment.

Guiding Principles for Cultivating Engagement

To encourage engagement with your students, here are a few guiding principles you ought to consider:

- Forge genuine connections with your students, understanding their unique strengths, challenges, and aspirations.
- Recognize and embrace the diversity of motivations within your classroom. Employ a spectrum of intrinsic and extrinsic motivators to cater to varied preferences.
- Let your enthusiasm for the subject matter shine through. Your passion becomes the fuel that propels engaging messages, creating a contagious atmosphere of curiosity and interest.
- Regularly assess the impact of your messages on student engagement. Adjust and refine your communication strategies based on ongoing observations and feedback.

Application Reflection

In the space below, share one innovative idea or strategy inspired by the AI-driven engagement tools discussed. How can you envision implementing it in your classroom to enhance student engagement?

AI Revolution in Education: Transforming Learning Landscapes in New Zealand and Beyond

In New Zealand, the integration of AI into the education system is transforming the traditional approach, offering tailored lessons and real-time feedback to students. Associate Professor Alex Sims from the University of Auckland sheds light on the evolving landscape of AI applications in education. While some schools grapple with the challenge of identifying bot-written work, Sims believes that AI can significantly benefit teachers by providing personalized responses to students' work.

Sims emphasizes the potential of AI to address challenges faced by students with dyslexia or those learning English as a second language. The current emphasis on writing skills in assessments often disadvantages these students, and Sims predicts a shift away from essay-based grading. AI, according to Sims, enables academics to offer personalized feedback amid the deluge of assignments, surpassing the capabilities of human writers.

Despite some resistance within academia to embrace AI, Sims envisions it as a valuable tool for tailoring lessons to meet individual student needs. Notably, AI-enabled generative tools are finding their way into curriculums, allowing students to verify and analyze answers produced by AI bots. As the prevalence of AI-generated content rises, plagiarism detection software faces new challenges and must evolve to identify AI-generated work accurately.

In New Zealand, the impact of AI on education has sparked discussions about reforming existing evaluation systems. Chris Whelan, Executive Director of Institutions New Zealand, advocates for a reconsideration of approaches to student evaluation, and Senior Lecturer Paul Geertsema from the University of Auckland echoes the sentiment, suggesting a reevaluation of essay requirements in light of AI's ability to produce high-quality articles.

The global recognition of AI's transformative potential extends to the Philippines and Indonesia. The University of the Philippines Mindanao and the Philippine Department of Science and Technology collaborate on an education program focused on AI, acknowledging its diverse applications. In Indonesia, the National Research and Innovation Agency recognizes AI's capacity to analyze external data, facilitating informed decision-making and progress toward targeted goals. As AI continues to advance, its influence on education and various sectors around the world is becoming increasingly evident (Santhika, 2023).

In this chapter, we explored the transformative power of AI in elevating student engagement. From adaptive learning platforms to gamified apps and virtual reality setups, we delved into practical tools and strategies that can redefine the classroom experience. Now, it's time to turn these insights into action.

Key Takeaways

- AI-driven tools offer personalized learning experiences catered to individual student needs.
- Strategies like gamification and virtual reality enhance student engagement and interest.
- Chatbots and AI-driven content recommendations provide real-time support and foster independent learning.
- Collecting student feedback is crucial to measuring the success of AI tools and tailoring instruction effectively.
- Observational data and AI analytics offer valuable insights into student behavior, participation, and progress.

Take a moment to reflect on how you can integrate these AI tools and strategies into your teaching approach. Consider experimenting with one or two concepts in your next class and observing the impact on student engagement.

As we journey deeper into the digital realm, the next chapter unveils how AI goes beyond engaging minds; it streamlines processes for peak classroom efficiency. Discover how AI becomes a teacher's best ally, providing more time for meaningful connections and shaping young minds. Engage with the evolving landscape of AI in education, where efficiency meets effectiveness. Stay tuned for insights that will revolutionize your teaching journey!

HELP SHAPE THE FUTURE OF EDUCATION

Be a Hero for Educators Everywhere

"Welcome to the future of education. It is like trying to catch a train that is already speeding down the tracks."

Would you lend a helping hand to a fellow educator, even if they were a stranger? Imagine someone just like you, or perhaps like you once were—eager to make a difference, seeking guidance, and searching for answers about how AI can benefit their teaching.

Our mission is to make AI in education accessible to every teacher. Everything we do at Teach Wise Publications revolves around that mission. To achieve it, we need to reach educators everywhere.

This is where you come in. People often judge a book by its cover (and its reviews). So here's my request on behalf of a teacher you've never met:

Please consider leaving a review for "AI-cademia—A Simplified Guide to AI for Educators." Your review won't cost you a dime and takes less than a minute, yet it can change a fellow teacher's teaching journey forever. Your review could help:

> ...another teacher better engage their students.
> ...a school improve its teaching methods.
> ...an educator gain confidence in using AI.
> ...a student receive a more personalized education.
> ...the future of education become brighter.

To leave your review, simply scan the QR code below:

If you believe in the power of education and want to make a difference in the lives of educators you've never met, you're our kind of person. Welcome to the club; you're one of us.

I'm thrilled to help you feel confident in navigating AI's applications in education. You'll find valuable insights in the upcoming chapters that will make AI a valuable tool in your teaching toolkit.

Thank you sincerely for your support. Let's continue shaping the future of education together!

- Your biggest fan, Teach Wise

PS - Did you know that providing value to someone makes you more valuable to them? If you think this book can help another educator, consider passing it along. Sharing knowledge is a powerful way to make a positive impact.

5

STREAMLINING THE CLASSROOM— A TEACHER'S GUIDE TO AI EFFICIENCY

"The first rule of any technology used in a business is that automation applied to an efficient operation will magnify the efficiency. The second is that automation applied to an inefficient operation will magnify the inefficiency."
–Bill Gate

So, now, let us translate this wisdom to the heart of education—the classroom. Imagine a future where efficiency is not just a goal but a reality, where the mundane tasks that consume your time are automated, allowing you to refocus on what truly matters: your students.

Delving into the aspect of AI efficiency, envision a classroom where administrative burdens are lifted and innovative teaching flourishes. The power of automation becomes a game-changer, creating an environment where educators can invest more in the growth and development of their students. Join us on this journey, where the synergy of education and technology propels us toward a more efficient and impactful teaching experience.

As you embark on this chapter's exploration into the efficiency revolution brought about by AI, let's kick things off with a reflective activity. Take a moment to jot down the time you currently dedicate to various teaching tasks in a typical week—grading, lesson planning, administrative duties, and any other significant responsibilities that fill your professional life.

Now, as we delve deeper into the transformative impact of AI on classroom efficiency, keep this time tracker handy. As you discover the myriad ways in which AI can streamline your teaching experience, revisit your tracker. Reflect on how these AI applications could potentially reshape your time allocation. Consider the possibilities of reclaiming valuable hours, making your teaching journey not just efficient but immensely rewarding.

The Era of Smart Classrooms

In this era of innovation, the integration of AI is revolutionizing the way educators teach and students learn. This has been partly facilitated by the emergence of smart classrooms.

A smart classroom is not just a physical space; it is an immersive educational environment that harnesses the capabilities of AI to enhance the learning experience. In a smart classroom, the walls seem to breathe with information, adapting to the needs of both educators and students. It goes beyond a tech upgrade; it's a paradigm shift in education.

In smart classrooms, static and one-size-fits-all teaching methods have become relics of the past. AI transforms learning spaces into interactive hubs, where lessons are customized to cater to individual student needs. Through adaptive learning platforms, students progress at their own pace, ensuring no one is left behind.

One of the cornerstones of the smart classroom is personalization. AI algorithms analyze each student's learning patterns and adapt content delivery accordingly. No two students are the same, and AI ensures that their educational journey reflects this diversity. It's education tailored to the individual, fostering a deeper understanding and mastery of subjects.

Gone are the days of waiting for assignments to be graded. Smart classrooms leverage AI for real-time feedback and assessment. Educators receive instant insights into student performance, allowing them to adjust their teaching strategies on the fly. Students benefit from immediate guidance, turning mistakes into learning opportunities.

The smart classroom is a hub of collaboration. AI facilitates seamless communication and interaction among students and educators. Virtual study groups, interactive projects, and global connections become not just possibilities but integral parts of the learning experience.

As an educator, envision a classroom where technology isn't a distraction but a powerful ally. The smart classroom prepares students for the challenges of tomorrow by instilling not only knowledge but also critical thinking, adaptability, and technological fluency.

Traditional Teaching vs. AI-Enhanced Learning

Let's take a stroll down the memory lane of traditional teaching and juxtapose it with the cutting-edge realm of AI-enhanced learning.

In the traditional system, we had a classic classroom with rows of students, all eyes on the teacher, scribbling on a chalkboard. The teacher, armed with textbooks and lesson plans, imparts knowledge to a sea of faces. One pace fits all, and personalized learning is just a distant dream.

Scene 1: One-Size-Fits-All Lectures

In the traditional setting, lessons are like monologues, where everyone receives the same information at the same pace. It is like serving a single dish at a banquet and hoping it suits every palate.

Scene 2: Manual Grading Nightmares

Fast forward to grading time—a mountain of papers to climb. Manual assessment is time-consuming, and students wait anxiously for feedback, often long after the assignment is forgotten.

Scene 3: Limited Interaction

Student engagement is a challenge. Shy students may hesitate to ask questions, and the classroom dynamic can be dominated by a vocal few. The struggle to ensure every student grasps the concept is real.

Now, let's step into the AI-enhanced world.

The smart classroom adapts to the needs of each student. The teacher is not just an instructor but a guide, and technology is not a distraction but a facilitator.

Scene 1: Personalized Learning Paths

In this dynamic space, AI tailors lessons to individual learning styles. Each student has a unique journey, progressing at their own pace. It's like having a personal tutor for every student, identifying strengths and weaknesses.

Scene 2: Real-Time Feedback Magic

Grading becomes a breeze with AI. Instant feedback is the name of the game. Students receive guidance while the lesson is fresh in their minds, turning mistakes into stepping stones for improvement.

Scene 3: Active Student Participation

AI fosters collaboration and interaction. Virtual study groups, interactive quizzes, and immersive experiences break down the barriers of shyness, making every student an active participant (Adarsh, 2023).

Quick question: Which scene resonates with you? The static script of traditional teaching or the dynamic, personalized experience of AI-enhanced learning? The choice is yours, and the future is now. As we dive into the AI-driven future, let's break the mold, challenge the norms, and create classrooms where every student thrives. The choice is yours—what kind of classroom will you build?

Efficient Classroom Management With AI

With the integration of AI within the spheres of education, your role as an educator is bound to become much easier with less fuss and more efficiency. Those who have been lucky enough to be around long enough can attest to the divergence and fluidity AI has channeled into the education ecosystem. As an educator, you can leverage the power of AI to seamlessly navigate many tasks within a short time and with a high degree of efficiency.

Automated Attendance Tracking

Say goodbye to the hassle of manual attendance-taking! With AI, tracking attendance becomes a breeze. With AI integration, the system instantly recognizes students as they enter the classroom. No more calling out names or sorting through papers. It's quick, accurate, and provides more time for meaningful interactions. Lately, several schools have implemented digital systems where learners' fingerprints are scanned to establish a record of daily attendance.

AI can employ facial recognition technology to identify students. As they walk in, the system registers their presence, ensuring accurate attendance records without consuming precious class time.

Smart Assignment Submissions

The days of drowning in a sea of papers are over. AI steps in to streamline assignment submissions. Students submit their work electronically, and the AI engine takes over. AI empowers you to create modules that students can conveniently access from any location. At the conclusion, they seamlessly transition into a timed assignment, eliminating the need for invigilation and traditional exam paper distribution. The future of education is efficient, accessible, and hassle-free.

AI does not just receive assignments; it provides instant feedback. Students receive constructive comments on their work immediately, allowing them to grasp concepts while the lesson is still fresh.

AI-Driven Behavior Monitoring

Maintaining an optimal learning environment is crucial. AI steps in as the silent guardian, monitoring class behavior and swiftly identifying disruptions.

Imagine an AI system that analyzes classroom behavior in real time. It recognizes patterns, ensuring a positive and focused learning environment. Any disruptions are promptly flagged, allowing you to address them on the spot.

Efficient classroom management means more time for impactful teaching. AI takes care of the administrative load, allowing you to focus on what truly matters—fostering connections and imparting knowledge.

Time-Saving AI Applications for Educators

In the current educational landscape, AI applications play a pivotal role in transforming traditional approaches. Today, you can experience the practical benefits of automating administrative tasks. From effortlessly grading assignments to receiving valuable suggestions for lesson plans, AI ensures efficiency in your daily responsibilities.

Moreover, welcome the convenience of virtual assistants specifically designed for teachers. These digital aides not only manage your schedule but also send timely reminders and recommend useful teaching resources. Embrace the reality of AI curating tailored content that seamlessly aligns with your curriculum requirements.

This is not a distant vision; it's the present reality. AI is here to revolutionize your teaching methods and time management.

As you navigate the vast landscape of AI tools, here are some standout platforms that can significantly enhance your teaching experience.

Bard

Bard utilizes natural language processing to craft original poetry and written content. Inject creativity into your language arts curriculum effortlessly, engaging students through unique and AI-generated content.

Canva

Canva offers user-friendly graphic design tools, enabling the creation of visually appealing presentations and resources.

Transform your teaching materials into visually captivating assets, elevating the overall aesthetic and impact of your lessons.

Curipod.com

Curipod.com leverages AI to restructure spoken content into organized study notes.

Expedite the note-taking process, providing students with well-organized study materials for improved comprehension.

SlidesGPT.com

SlidesGPT.com revolutionizes presentation creation through AI-generated slides.

Save time by crafting visually engaging slideshows, allowing you to focus on delivering impactful lessons.

Conker.ai

Conker.ai employs AI for content analysis, aiding educators in understanding student engagement and learning patterns.

Gain insights into your student's progress and adapt your teaching methods based on real-time analytics for a more personalized approach.

Otter.ai

Otter.ai utilizes AI-driven transcription services to convert spoken words into text with high accuracy.

Simplify the process of transcribing lectures and discussions, saving time on manual note-taking and ensuring accurate records.

myViewBoard.com

myViewBoard.com is an interactive whiteboard platform incorporating AI for collaborative and engaging virtual classrooms.

Foster interactive and dynamic learning environments, promoting student participation and comprehension through the power of AI-enhanced visuals.

Runwayml.com

Runwayml.com enables educators to explore and integrate machine learning models into various creative projects.

Introduce students to the world of machine learning in a user-friendly manner, encouraging creativity and innovation in diverse academic disciplines.

Adobe Firefly

Adobe Firefly is an AI-powered platform designed to enhance the creation and delivery of educational content, offering tools for interactive lessons, assessments, and collaboration.

Empower your teaching with multimedia-rich content creation and interactive assessments, fostering a dynamic and engaging learning atmosphere.

Teachmateai.com

Teachmateai.com leverages AI to provide personalized tutoring and learning support to students based on their individual needs and learning styles.

Tailor your teaching approach by incorporating personalized learning pathways, allowing students to receive targeted assistance and guidance.

Integrate these tools into your teaching toolkit and witness the transformation of your classroom into a dynamic and personalized learning space.

Teachers Harnessing the Power of AI

Meet Jessica Reid, a dedicated elementary school teacher and a mother of three who once found herself on the brink of abandoning her lifelong dream due to the overwhelming workload. The struggle of planning lessons, managing behavioral support plans, grading, and juggling family responsibilities left her questioning her ability to do justice to both her students and her own family.

However, a turning point arrived when Jessica decided to explore the realm of artificial intelligence to streamline her teaching responsibilities. Joining the ranks of educators embracing technology, she sought AI tools to make her workload more manageable, especially with the anticipation of a new school year.

"I really wanted to dedicate this summer to exploring some of these AI tools and how they help me in my planning and my administrative duties," she shared from her home in Muskoka, Ont (Thompson, 2023). The dilemma of sacrificing family time for endless planning or feeling inadequate in her teaching compelled Jessica to seek a solution that could strike a balance.

Jessica's newfound ally in education is an AI program named Eduaide.Ai. Instead of relying on it for information, she uses it to generate lesson plans, providing her with a guideline of what to teach and when. "I was able to plan most of my school year in a really short amount of time this summer," she said (Thompson, 2023). The AI seamlessly filled in gaps in subjects where she lacked expertise or passion.

Excited by her discoveries, Jessica took to social media to share her experiences and resources. However, her innovative approach sparked both support and criticism. Some questioned the ethical implications, arguing that students might perceive it as cheating.

Yet, Jessica dismisses these concerns, emphasizing the fundamental difference between the role of a teacher and a student. "I earned my role as a teacher. I already have been through the education system," she asserted (Thompson, 2023).

The story of Jessica Reid echoes a broader sentiment among educators. The rise of AI in education elicits both skepticism and excitement. While concerns about potential student misuse exist, teachers like Kasi Humber in Truro, Nova Scotia, see AI as a disruptive force that can enhance efficiency.

Kasi, a French teacher, embraced AI after the release of ChatGPT, an AI-powered language model. She incorporated it into her routine to streamline report card creation, enabling her to organize grades and comments efficiently. Additionally, Kasi leveraged AI to provide personalized reading materials tailored to her students' levels and interests, effectively enhancing their reading comprehension.

The journey of Jessica and Kasi exemplifies the transformative power of AI in education, where technology becomes a valuable ally for educators striving to navigate the ever-evolving landscape of teaching (Thompson, 2023).

In this chapter, we navigated the transformative landscape of AI in education, focusing on the pivotal theme of streamlining classroom efficiency. From smart classrooms to time-saving applications, we unraveled the possibilities of AI, magnifying the effectiveness of every educator's efforts.

Key Takeaways

- AI offers a gateway to automating administrative tasks, grading, and lesson planning, liberating educators from mundane chores.
- We explored the concept of smart classrooms, where AI seamlessly integrates to enhance the teaching and learning experience.
- AI applications act as virtual assistants, aiding in schedule management, reminders, and personalized content curation, allowing educators to focus on what truly matters.
- Delving into a toolbox of AI wonders, we introduced tools like Bard, Canva, Curipod.com, SlidesGPT.com, Conker.ai, Otter.ai, myViewBoard.com, Runwayml.com, Adobe Firefly, and

Teachmateai.com, showcasing their unique features and efficiency-boosting capabilities.

Now, it's your turn to harness the power of AI in your teaching journey. Revisit your time tracker and envision how these AI applications can reshape your routine. Take the plunge, experiment, and witness first-hand the revolution AI brings to your classroom efficiency. As you implement these strategies, you are not just embracing technology; you are crafting a future where your time is maximized for impactful student interactions and personalized instruction.

Having tapped into the efficiency AI offers in the classroom, it is time to set our sights on the broader horizon of innovation. As teachers, it is not just about reacting to AI developments but also about steering the course of the future of education. How can we stay at the forefront of AI's evolution and make informed choices that reshape the learning landscape?

In the upcoming chapter, we will embark on a journey beyond the classroom, exploring how educators can proactively engage with AI advancements. Discover strategies to not only keep up with the latest AI trends but also to wield this powerful tool to shape the educational frontier. Join us as we delve into the proactive side of AI integration, ensuring that you, as an educator, become a trailblazer in the AI-driven educational landscape.

6

SURFING THE AI WAVE—STAYING ABREAST OF AI DEVELOPMENTS

"Change is the only constant."
–Heraclitus

In the realm of AI, this change is lightning-fast. For educators, staying updated is not just a choice; it is a necessity to remain effective and relevant.

In this chapter, we dive headfirst into the dynamic world of AI advancements. As technology evolves at an unprecedented pace, you must not only ride the wave but also learn to surf it skillfully. The goal is not merely to keep up with AI developments but to proactively navigate this ever-changing landscape, ensuring that you are not just spectators but active participants in shaping the future of education.

Methods to Keep Up with AI Advancements

In the ever-evolving landscape of education technology, keeping pace with AI advancements is not just a choice for educators—it is a critical necessity. As the boundaries of what AI can achieve in education continue to expand, staying informed becomes paramount for educators to harness the full potential of these transformative tools. This section delves into compelling ways to stay current on these advancements.

Conferences and Workshops

Going to conferences about AI in education is really important for teachers. It's not just about learning new things; it's like diving into a big pool of opportunities that AI can bring to education.

Imagine going to a conference where you do not just listen to talks but also get to try things out. It is like a workshop where you can actually use AI tools and see how they work. It is not just talking about ideas; it is doing things and seeing how AI can change education.

Moreover, the people that you meet at these conferences are not just there to say hello and exchange numbers. They are experts in the field, the ones leading the way in AI and education. Talking to them is like being part of the big conversation about how AI is shaping education.

The rationale for attending these conferences surpasses the notion of fulfilling a professional development requirement. It constitutes a strategic initiative aimed at infusing teaching practices with the latest insights from AI, refining skills through participatory workshops, and establishing connections with thought leaders steering the revolution in AI-driven education. Attending such conferences becomes imperative not merely to keep pace with the evolving wave of AI but to navigate and harness its capabilities with assurance and purpose adeptly.

Each year, Boston hosts a significant AI in Education conference that draws educators from around the world. This event serves as a unique platform for global educators to come together, sharing their diverse experiences and learning from leading experts in the field.

The conference provides a space for educators to discuss the various ways AI is impacting education in their respective regions. It is not just about listening to lectures; it is a collaborative environment where teachers can exchange ideas, strategies, and success stories related to integrating AI into their classrooms.

Moreover, the conference features sessions led by prominent experts, offering valuable insights into the latest advancements and best practices in AI education. Attendees have the opportunity to participate in discussions, workshops, and hands-on activities that enhance their understanding and implementation of AI tools in diverse educational settings.

The annual gathering in Boston has become a hub for fostering a global community of educators passionate about leveraging AI to enhance teaching and learning. It exemplifies the power of collaboration and knowledge-sharing, ultimately contributing to the continuous improvement of educational practices worldwide.

Online Courses

In your quest to stay informed about the latest advancements in AI within education, consider enrolling in online courses specifically designed to equip you with this knowledge.

Attending online courses offers a flexible and accessible way for you to deepen your understanding of AI applications in education. These courses often cover a range of topics, from the basics of AI technology to its practical implementation in educational settings. As you engage with the course material, you gain insights into the latest trends, methodologies, and innovative approaches that can be directly applied in your teaching environments.

Platforms such as Coursera, Udemy, and edX play a pivotal role in facilitating educators' access to valuable courses related to AI in education. These online learning platforms offer a diverse range of courses that cater to educators with varying levels of expertise and interests.

One key advantage of these platforms is their accessibility. Educators can enroll in courses from anywhere in the world, providing them with the flexibility to learn at their own pace and schedule. This accessibility is particularly beneficial for busy educators who may find it challenging to attend traditional, location-based courses.

Coursera, Udemy, and edX host a multitude of courses on AI in education, covering topics such as machine learning applications, data analysis for educational insights, and the integration of AI tools into the learning environment. These courses are often developed and led by experts in the field, ensuring high-quality content and relevance to current trends.

One of the standout courses on Coursera that has proven immensely beneficial for thousands of educators worldwide is "AI for Everyone" by Andrew Ng. This course, developed by the co-founder of Coursera and a renowned AI expert, offers a nontechnical introduction to the fundamentals of artificial intelligence (Coursera, n.d.).

Andrew Ng's "AI for Everyone" provides a comprehensive overview of AI concepts, technologies, and their potential impact on various industries, including education. Educators who have taken this course commend its clarity in explaining complex AI topics, making it accessible to individuals without a technical background.

The course covers key AI principles, ethical considerations, and real-world applications, offering valuable insights you can directly apply to your teaching environments. Its popularity stems from its ability to empower educators with the knowledge needed to navigate the AI landscape and integrate these technologies thoughtfully into their classrooms.

Moreover, these platforms frequently offer both free and paid courses, allowing educators to choose based on their preferences and budget constraints. The variety of courses available ensures that educators can find content suitable for their specific needs, whether they are beginners looking for foundational knowledge or experienced practitioners seeking advanced insights.

By actively participating in such online courses, you can not only enhance your knowledge of AI but also stay ahead of developments, ensuring you remain well-informed and capable of integrating cutting-edge technologies into your teaching practices.

Educational Journals

In our journey to stay ahead of the curve in the dynamic world of AI, subscribing to reputable AI research journals emerges as a crucial compass. These educational journals serve as beacons guiding us through the latest academic advancements, ensuring we are well-informed and ready to adapt.

By regularly delving into respected AI research journals, you equip yourself with insights into groundbreaking studies, emerging trends, and innovative practices within the realm of education and artificial intelligence. These journals provide a platform for scholars, experts, and practitioners to share their findings, contributing to a collective pool of knowledge that elevates our understanding of AI's role in education.

Subscribing to these journals is akin to opening a window to the forefront of AI research. It allows you to explore in-depth analyses, methodologies, and critical discussions that shape the current landscape and future trajectories of AI in education. By immersing yourself in the academic discourse, you not only stay informed but also become an active participant in the ongoing dialogue that propels our field forward.

Exploring the realms of AI education is an enriching journey, and one valuable resource to navigate this dynamic landscape is the Journal of Artificial Intelligence Research (JAIR). This esteemed journal is committed to swiftly disseminating crucial research findings across the global AI community. JAIR's comprehensive scope spans various domains within AI, encompassing agents and multi-agent systems, automated reasoning, constraint processing and search, knowledge representation, machine learning, natural language, planning and scheduling, robotics and vision, and the intricacies of uncertainty in the field of AI.

Within the rich tapestry of JAIR, you'll find a wealth of insights and discoveries that unravel the complexities of AI, shedding light on the latest advancements and innovative applications. Whether you're delving into the intricacies of machine learning, exploring the realms of natural language processing, or seeking a deeper understanding of robotics and vision, JAIR stands as a beacon of knowledge, providing a platform for thought-provoking research and discussions (The Journal of Artificial Intelligence Research, 2023).

As an educator navigating the burgeoning landscape of AI in education, consider JAIR as a guiding compass, offering you access to cutting-edge research that can inform and elevate your pedagogical practices. The journal's commitment to inclusivity ensures that it caters to diverse facets of AI, making it a valuable repository of information that transcends boundaries and fosters a collaborative and informed AI community.

Saikumar Talari, an AI enthusiast and expert, curates a list of six AI subscriptions that serve as invaluable resources in keeping you abreast of the latest developments and trends in the field (Talari, 2018).

The Algorithm

Aiming to demystify the complex world of algorithms, *The Algorithm* provides insightful content that caters to both beginners and seasoned AI enthusiasts. Whether you are delving into the basics or exploring advanced algorithmic concepts, this subscription promises a wealth of knowledge.

Open Data Science Conference (ODSC)

ODSC is more than just a conference; it is a dynamic platform that offers ongoing insights into the expansive domain of data science and AI. Subscribing to *ODSC* ensures you receive a steady stream of resources, including articles, webinars, and event updates, keeping you connected with the evolving landscape of AI.

O'Reilly AI

Recognized for its authoritative content and in-depth publications, *O'Reilly AI* provides a subscription that delivers high-quality learning resources. From comprehensive books to thought-provoking articles, this subscription is designed to cater to AI practitioners seeking both breadth and depth in their understanding.

Data Elixir

For a curated selection of data science and AI news, *Data Elixir* is a go-to subscription. Tailored to deliver a digestible yet comprehensive overview of the latest happenings, this resource keeps you informed without overwhelming your inbox, making it an efficient choice for busy educators.

AI Weekly

As the name suggests, *AI Weekly* is a newsletter that condenses the week's most noteworthy AI developments into a concise and accessible format. Subscribing to *AI Weekly* ensures you stay informed without dedicating excessive time to scouring multiple sources.

Import AI

Known for its meticulous curation of AI-related content, *Import AI* offers a subscription that brings a blend of research papers, news, and commentary directly to your inbox. This resource is ideal for those seeking a deeper dive into the technical aspects of AI.

Networking

Joining AI-centric educational groups on platforms like LinkedIn provides a dynamic space for knowledge exchange and professional growth.

As an educator navigating the realms of AI, being part of these groups opens doors to a vast community of like-minded professionals. Engaging in discussions, sharing insights, and posing queries allow you to tap into a collective pool of experiences. Whether you are seeking advice on implementing AI tools in the classroom or staying updated on the latest trends, these groups serve as invaluable resources.

Imagine connecting with educators who have successfully integrated AI into their teaching methodologies. Picture the potential collaborations, shared resources, and firsthand accounts of challenges and triumphs.

LinkedIn groups dedicated to AI in education become virtual hubs where educators converge to discuss, learn, and inspire.

Furthermore, these groups often host webinars, events, and virtual meetups, providing opportunities to interact with industry experts, thought leaders, and fellow educators. The connections forged in these spaces can extend beyond the digital realm, fostering relationships that transcend geographic boundaries.

Podcasts and Webinars

In the fast-paced world of education and artificial intelligence (AI), staying informed has never been more accessible, thanks to the convenience of podcasts and webinars. These audio and visual mediums serve as on-the-go companions, transforming your commute, workout, or downtime into valuable learning experiences.

The upside of podcasts is that you can get plugged into an AI-focused podcast while commuting to work. In the span of a single episode, you gain insights into emerging AI trends, innovative teaching methodologies, and real-world applications. The auditory format allows you to absorb information effortlessly, making it a seamless addition to your daily routine.

For an illuminating exploration of artificial intelligence in the contemporary landscape, I highly recommend tuning in to the AI Today podcast hosted by Kathleen Walch and Ronald Schmelzer. In this podcast, the dynamic duo from *Cognilytica* delivers insightful discussions and easily digestible content on the latest developments in the realm of artificial intelligence (Walch, 2018).

Diving into pressing topics surrounding AI, the hosts engage with interview guests and subject matter experts to provide listeners with a comprehensive understanding of the current state of AI adoption and implementation. The podcast stands out for its ability to cut through the noise and hype, offering a clear and informed perspective on the real happenings in the dynamic world of artificial intelligence.

Webinars, on the other hand, provide a visual feast of knowledge. Imagine joining a live session where industry experts discuss the latest advancements in AI and their implications for education. The interactive nature of webinars allows you to pose questions, participate in discussions, and glean practical strategies for integrating AI tools into your teaching arsenal.

The beauty of podcasts and webinars lies in their flexibility. Whether you're grading papers, going for a jog, or sipping your morning coffee, you can effortlessly stay connected with the ever-evolving landscape of AI in education. It's professional development at your fingertips, tailored to your schedule and preferences.

A Checklist for You

As an educator navigating this digital frontier, it's crucial to familiarize yourself with the diverse applications of AI that are at your disposal. The checklist below serves as your comprehensive guide, detailing various AI tools and features you may encounter in your daily routine or research pursuits. Consider this checklist your personal roadmap, allowing you to track the AI tools you come across and fostering a continual journey of exploration and adaptation in the realm of AI-powered education (University of San Diego, 2021).

- adaptive learning platforms
- gamified learning apps
- virtual reality setups
- chatbots for homework assistance
- AI-driven content recommendations
- AI-enhanced grading systems
- virtual class attendance tracking
- smart assignment submission and feedback
- AI-driven behavior monitoring
- administrative task automation tools
- virtual assistants for teachers
- tailored content curation tools
- Canva for AI-enhanced graphics
- Curipod.com for customizable learning pods
- SlidesGPT.com for AI-generated presentations
- Conker.ai for collaborative learning
- Otter.ai for AI-powered transcription

- myViewBoard.com for interactive whiteboards
- runwayml.com for creative AI projects
- Adobe Firefly for document collaboration
- Teachmateai.com for AI-assisted teaching

In this chapter, we embarked on a journey to understand the imperative of staying abreast of AI developments in the ever-evolving landscape of education. Our key takeaway? Staying updated isn't merely a choice for educators; it's a necessity to remain effective and relevant in shaping the future of education.

Now armed with insights into various methods of staying updated with AI advancements, it's time to turn knowledge into action. Attend conferences, enroll in online courses, delve into educational journals, and explore the wealth of resources available. Equip yourself with the tools needed to not just keep up but to lead the way in leveraging AI for enhanced teaching and learning experiences.

Having scratched the surface of AI research, the next part of our journey dives even deeper. In Chapter 7, you will learn how to maintain stability in the ever-changing, AI-powered world of education. Are you ready to jump in and navigate the waves of innovation? Get set for a comprehensive guide on mastering stability in the AI-powered classroom.

7

SEIZING THE FUTURE—PREPARING FOR AN AI-INFUSED EDUCATION LANDSCAPE

"The best way to predict the future is to invent it."
−Alan Kay

As educators, we stand at the forefront of shaping the classroom of the future. In this fast-evolving landscape where AI plays a pivotal role, how do we proactively prepare for the seismic shifts and opportunities that lie ahead? This chapter is your guide to seizing the future, offering actionable strategies to not only embrace but also thrive in an education landscape driven by the transformative power of AI. The question beckons: How will you prepare for the educational paradigm of tomorrow? Let us dive in and explore the possibilities.

The Long-Term Vision of AI in Education

In envisioning the future landscape of education, AI emerges as a powerful force with the potential to revolutionize classrooms, redefine teaching methodologies, and enhance the overall learning experience. The inspiration for this transformative journey lies in harnessing the capabilities of AI to facilitate not just more but higher-quality human learning interactions. Instead of replacing teachers, AI is poised to support educators and the education system through the automation of tasks and the development of stimulating problems.

Teacher and AI Collaboration

A symbiotic relationship between teachers and AI is envisaged, where educators act as filters for useful suggestions generated by AI. This collaboration aims to empower teachers by leveraging AI tools for tasks such as grading and student tracking, allowing them to focus more on fostering meaningful interactions with their students.

AI-Generated Inspiring Problems

AI's role extends to the creation and dissemination of captivating problems in local educational contexts. Drawing inspiration from machine learning's ability to create art, the question arises: Can AI algorithms generate engaging, personalized activities? This synthesis of human and artificial intelligence establishes a dynamic teaching and learning ecosystem, emphasizing social and emotional interactions.

Low-Data Feedback

Embracing the concept of low-data AI, the focus is on providing meaningful feedback for inspiring, open-ended assignments without relying on massive student datasets. This approach minimizes the risks associated with data abuse and ensures practicality in implementing AI-driven feedback on creative, exploratory tasks.

Understanding Process

AI's current effectiveness lies in teaching structured lessons, but ongoing research explores its potential to understand the learning process rather than just the final product. This model envisions AI-powered tools working alongside teachers to monitor and analyze the learning process, positioning educators as coaches and mentors in the educational journey.

AI for Translation of Educational Content

Addressing the issue of uneven distribution of educational content, AI, specifically natural language processing, can play a pivotal role in supporting translation efforts. By providing inclusive education in low-resource languages, AI contributes to the development of educational technology tailored to local communities.

AI-Powered Risk Detection for Child Safety

Acknowledging the importance of safety in online learning spaces, AI is called upon to develop scalable content moderation tools. This ensures a secure environment for learners, particularly children and those in vulnerable contexts, protecting them from harmful content (Piech & Einstein, 2020).

As we explore these advancements, it becomes clear that while AI holds immense potential for joyful learning, addressing concerns and ensuring responsible deployment are paramount. The collective responsibility of the education policy community and AI researchers is to consider the diverse applications of these technologies and actively engage the public in conversations about potential harms and strategies for promoting human flourishing.

Revolutionizing Education With AI: Personalized Learning, Accessibility, and Global Impact

AI emerges as a transformative force, promising to reshape the very foundations of personalized learning, accessibility, and global education.

Personalized Learning Redefined

Imagine a classroom where AI acts as a virtual assistant, understanding the individual needs and learning styles of each student. Through continuous assessment and data analysis, AI tailors educational content, pacing, and activities to suit the specific requirements of learners. The result is an educational experience that not only meets students where they are but propels them forward on their unique academic paths.

Enhanced Accessibility

AI holds the promise of breaking down barriers to education, ensuring that learning opportunities are accessible to all, irrespective of geographical location, socio-economic status, or physical abilities. Language barriers can be overcome with AI-driven translation tools, and content can be adapted to suit diverse cultural contexts, fostering an inclusive and equitable educational environment.

Global Collaboration in Education

Imagine a world where classrooms are not confined by physical borders. AI facilitates real-time collaboration among students and educators from different parts of the globe. Language is no longer a hindrance, as AI translation ensures seamless communication. This interconnectedness opens up a wealth of perspectives, enriching the educational experience by exposing learners to diverse cultures, ideas, and approaches to problem-solving.

As educators, the potential impact of AI on personalized learning, accessibility, and global education is both promising and profound. Embracing these advancements requires us to not only adapt our teaching methodologies but also actively contribute to shaping the ethical considerations surrounding AI in education.

Preparation Strategies for Educators

To truly excel as an educator and fulfill the dynamic needs of the modern classroom, embodying the spirit of a lifelong learner is not merely advantageous; it is an essential mindset. The concept of lifelong learning extends beyond the confines of traditional academic settings, transcending the completion of formal degrees or the boundaries of a classroom. It signifies a commitment to continuous growth, exploration, and adaptation, acknowledging that the educational landscape is ever-evolving (Kimmons, 2020).

As a teacher, your journey as a lifelong learner begins the moment you step out of the classroom or earn that degree. It is an ongoing process of discovery and refinement, fueled by an insatiable curiosity about the world, emerging pedagogies, and advancements in technology. Lifelong learning becomes the compass, where each new piece of knowledge gained is a building block for enhanced teaching practices and enriched student engagement.

Why is this mindset crucial, especially in the context of technological advancements? The answer lies in the transformative impact that AI can have on the educational landscape. Lifelong learning equips you with the tools not only to adapt to these changes but also to harness them to enhance your teaching methods, engage your students more effectively, and ultimately elevate the quality of education you provide.

Consider it your personal superpower—a commitment to staying curious, open-minded, and proactive in seeking out new skills and insights. Lifelong learning empowers you to decipher the complexities of emerging technologies, making you not just a consumer but a contributor to the educational advancements of tomorrow.

By adopting the mindset of a lifelong learner, you position yourself as a leader in the ever-expanding realm of educational technology. You become an agile and adaptive educator, ready to leverage the full potential of tools like AI to create enriching learning experiences for your students. Your journey as a lifelong learner is not just about keeping up; it is about being at the forefront of shaping the future of education.

As you embark on your journey of incorporating technology into your teaching methods, consider the following recommendations to navigate this dynamic intersection of education and technology.

Forge Partnerships with Tech Experts

Establishing partnerships with tech experts within your school community or through external networks can be invaluable. These collaborations provide you with insights into the latest technological trends, guidance on implementation, and troubleshooting support when integrating new tools into your teaching repertoire.

Participate in Professional Development Opportunities

Stay informed about professional development opportunities that focus on educational technology. Attend workshops, webinars, and conferences that bring together educators and tech experts. These events provide a platform for knowledge exchange, allowing you to learn from the experiences of others and gain practical insights into effective tech integration.

Engage in Online Communities

Joining online communities or forums dedicated to education and technology creates a virtual space for collaboration. Platforms like social media groups, forums, and educational networks allow you to connect with tech-savvy educators, share ideas, seek advice, and stay updated on the latest tech advancements relevant to education.

Regularly Check Tech News Sources

Keeping abreast of tech news is crucial for understanding the broader technological landscape. Follow reputable tech news sources, blogs, and publications that cover advancements in educational technology. Regularly checking these sources ensures you stay informed about emerging tools, trends, and potential applications in the education sector.

Attend Tech Conferences

Attend conferences specifically focused on technology in education. These events often feature keynotes, panel discussions, and interactive sessions led by tech experts. Participating in such conferences not only provides exposure to cutting-edge technologies but also offers opportunities to network with professionals driving innovation in the field.

Tech-Infused Classrooms: A Futuristic Blend of Learning and Innovation

The collaboration of technology has ushered in a new era, transforming traditional classrooms into digital hubs of learning. As we explore this intersection of education and technology, let's delve into key aspects that are shaping the educational sector and revolutionizing the way we teach and students learn.

Digital Classrooms

The traditional chalk-and-board setup has given way to interactive digital classrooms. These digital spaces leverage multimedia elements, allowing educators to present information in engaging formats such as videos, interactive slideshows, and real-time collaboration tools.

Impact of AR/VR Technologies on eLearning

Augmented reality (AR) and VR technologies have made a significant impact on eLearning. These immersive technologies transport students to virtual environments, providing hands-on experiences that enhance understanding and retention of complex concepts.

Cloud Computing for Seamless Data Sharing

Cloud computing has revolutionized data storage and sharing in education. Teachers and students can access learning materials and collaborate on projects from anywhere, fostering seamless communication and information sharing.

Ubiquity of Smart Devices

The widespread use of smartphones, tablets, and laptops has created a tech-savvy learning environment. These devices serve as powerful tools for accessing educational content, engaging with interactive apps, and fostering a more personalized learning experience.

Audiobooks and Video Conferencing

Audiobooks offer an alternative method of content consumption, catering to diverse learning preferences. Additionally, video conferencing tools facilitate virtual classrooms, enabling real-time interaction between educators and students, regardless of geographical distances.

eLearning Apps

The rise of eLearning apps has provided students with convenient access to educational resources. These apps cover a spectrum of subjects, offering interactive lessons, quizzes, and personalized learning paths tailored to individual student needs.

Gamified Learning

Gamification has injected an element of fun into learning. Educational games and gamified platforms leverage the principles of game design to make learning engaging and enjoyable, motivating students to participate actively in the educational process.

As you navigate this digital collaboration in the educational sector, consider how these technological advancements can be harnessed to create a vibrant and effective learning environment. Embrace the opportunities technology brings to engage your students, foster collaboration, and inspire a love for learning.

Sketching the Future of AI-Enhanced Learning

Take a moment to envision your ideal AI-infused classroom. What elements would make learning more engaging, personalized, and effective for your students? Use this space to sketch or jot down your thoughts. Revisit this annually to reflect on the changes, innovations, and perhaps even surprises that unfold. Embrace the opportunity to shape the future of education through your creative insights and proactive mindset.

- _____
- _____
- _____
- _____
- _____
- _____
- _____
- _____
- _____
- _____
- _____
- _____
- _____
- _____
- _____
- _____
- _____
- _____

As we conclude this chapter, it is crucial to reinforce the key takeaways. The future of education is undeniably intertwined with AI, and as educators, embracing this evolution is not just beneficial—it's imperative. The strategies discussed here are not mere suggestions; they are actionable steps to prepare for the imminent changes in our classrooms.

Now is the time to put these ideas into action. Consider sketching your vision for an AI-enhanced classroom, collaborating with tech experts, and immersing yourself in digital collaboration tools. Become a lifelong learner, attend conferences, and explore AI applications that resonate with your teaching style. Your commitment to adapting and evolving will define the success of your educational journey.

In the upcoming chapter, we will explore a fascinating intersection: how AI technologies are reshaping homeschooling and redefining personalized learning. As we delve into the convergence of traditional schooling and home education, prepare to witness the transformative impact AI can have on tailoring education to individual needs. Join us on this enlightening journey, and let's explore the limitless possibilities together!

8

HOMESCHOOLING IN THE AGE OF AI—UNLEASHING THE POWER OF PERSONALIZED LEARNING

As we embark on this enlightening journey, keep in mind the timeless wisdom of Socrates: "Education is the kindling of a flame, not the filling of a vessel" (Socrates, n.d.). Picture every vessel as unique, each seeking its own distinct spark. In the realm of homeschooling, AI isn't just about embracing modernity; it's about honoring individuality.

The goal is to ascertain that you will gain a profound appreciation for how AI can transform the homeschooling landscape. There are a vast number of specific AI tools and strategies designed to cater to individual student needs and help you unlock an enriched and personalized learning journey. Whether you're a seasoned homeschooling teacher or just beginning to explore this educational path, get ready to discover the limitless possibilities AI can bring to the heart of your home.

Benefits of AI in Homeschooling Environments

In homeschooling, the integration of AI offers myriad benefits that contribute to a richer and more personalized learning experience.

Here are some key advantages:

1. **Adaptive learning resources:** AI algorithms can analyze a students' performance and adapt learning resources accordingly. If a student excels in a particular subject, the system can provide more challenging material while additional support is offered for areas where the student may struggle.
2. **Immediate feedback:** AI enables real-time assessment and feedback. Students receive instant evaluation on their assignments and quizzes, allowing them to grasp concepts more

effectively and make corrections promptly. This is a game-changer because homeschooling inherently allows for immediate feedback, and now, with the infusion of AI integration, it becomes even more seamless and efficient.
3. **Engaging educational content:** AI technologies can generate interactive and engaging content, such as educational games, simulations, and virtual reality experiences. This dynamic content not only captures students' interest but also enhances their understanding of complex concepts.
4. **Time efficiency:** AI streamlines administrative tasks for homeschooling parents, freeing up more time for direct interaction with their children. Automated grading, lesson planning suggestions, and progress tracking provide a more efficient homeschooling environment.
5. **Access to global resources:** AI facilitates access to a wealth of educational resources and materials worldwide. This global perspective enriches the learning experience, exposing students to diverse cultures, ideas, and perspectives.
6. **Social and emotional support:** AI tools can incorporate social and emotional learning components into the curriculum, promoting holistic development. Virtual tutors or chatbots equipped with emotional intelligence can provide additional support beyond academic subjects (Graham, 2023).

AI-Driven Games to Keep Your Students Engaged

As you embark on the homeschooling journey, consider the exciting realm of AI-driven educational games that go beyond mere entertainment. These games are crafted to captivate students' attention while effectively imparting complex concepts. They facilitate a learning environment where your child or student is not just absorbing information but actively engaging with interactive games that make education a thrilling adventure.

Here are examples of AI-driven educational games that can captivate students while teaching complex concepts:

DragonBox Numbers

- Concepts taught: Fundamental math skills
- This game uses a visually appealing and interactive interface to teach children essential math concepts, making learning arithmetic a fun experience

Minecraft: Education Edition

- Concepts taught: Creativity, problem-solving, and collaboration
- While not exclusively AI-driven, Minecraft incorporates elements of artificial intelligence to create an immersive and adaptive learning environment. It encourages students to explore, create, and collaborate on various projects

Algo Bot

- Concepts taught: Basics of coding and algorithms
- Algo Bot introduces programming concepts in a game format. Players solve puzzles by giving commands to robots, providing a hands-on introduction to coding principles

Brain Age: Concentration Training

- Concepts taught: Cognitive skills and memory improvement
- This game uses AI algorithms to adapt difficulty levels based on the player's performance. It offers a variety of challenges to enhance concentration, memory, and overall cognitive abilities

Squirrel AI

- Concepts taught: Personalized learning across multiple subjects
- Squirrel AI is an adaptive learning platform that uses AI to tailor lessons based on individual student needs. It covers a range of subjects, providing a customized learning experience

These examples showcase the diverse ways in which AI-driven educational games can make learning both enjoyable and effective for students in a homeschooling environment.

Adaptive Learning With AI: Tailoring the Learning Pace

In the realm of homeschooling, AI serves as a dynamic tool capable of adapting the pace of learning to meet the unique needs of each student. This adaptability ensures that educational experiences are personalized, promoting a deeper understanding of concepts and accommodating different learning speeds.

Let's explore practical tips and tools to integrate AI seamlessly into your homeschooling journey.

- Engage in meaningful discussions with your child to collaboratively set learning goals. Leverage AI platforms that facilitate goal setting based on individual strengths, weaknesses, and interests. This fosters a sense of ownership in the learning process.
- Explore a myriad of AI-powered educational apps and tools designed to make learning interactive and engaging. Platforms like Khan Academy, Duolingo, and Squirrel AI offer adaptive learning experiences, tailoring content to your child's proficiency level and providing real-time feedback.
- Utilize AI-powered tools to track your child's progress comprehensively. These tools offer insights into areas of strength and areas that may need additional focus. Adaptive assessments, such as those provided by DreamBox or Smart Sparrow, can be valuable allies in gauging development (Alecia, 2023).

Seamlessly integrating AI into your homeschooling routine with these tips and tools empowers your child with a personalized and effective learning experience. The adaptive nature of AI ensures that education aligns with your child's unique learning journey.

Tools and Strategies Tailored for Homeschool Educators

These tools harness the power of artificial intelligence to create exercises that cater to specific proficiency levels, providing a more effective and engaging way for students to grasp complex concepts.

- **Khan Academy:** Khan Academy offers personalized learning experiences in various subjects. The platform uses adaptive technology to adjust the difficulty of exercises based on a student's progress, ensuring a customized and paced learning journey.
- **Smart Sparrow:** Smart Sparrow's adaptive e-learning platform utilizes AI to create personalized exercises and assessments. It adapts to students' responses, providing targeted feedback and adjusting the difficulty of the content to match their proficiency.
- **IXL Learning:** IXL is an online learning platform that uses AI to create adaptive quizzes and exercises for students. It covers a range of subjects and adjusts the difficulty level based on individual performance.
- **AdaptiveU:** AdaptiveU is an AI-powered platform that personalizes learning paths for students. It analyzes their strengths and weaknesses, offering tailored exercises and content to enhance understanding.

These tools leverage AI to enhance the homeschooling experience by providing personalized exercises aligned with each student's unique learning requirements.

In the dynamic homeschooling landscape, leveraging AI to adapt lessons to your child's pace can be a game-changer. Several platforms have embraced this innovative approach, ensuring that learning is personalized and paced according to each student's individual needs.

AI for Personalized Pacing

One notable category of platforms is adaptive learning systems, which utilize AI algorithms to dynamically adjust the difficulty and pace of lessons. These platforms observe a student's progress, identify areas of strength and weakness, and tailor the curriculum accordingly.

Here are some examples of platforms that you may leverage:

Assessment and Learning in Knowledge Spaces (ALEKS)

ALEKS stands out as an adaptive learning platform that harnesses the power of artificial intelligence AI to revolutionize the educational experience for students. Unlike traditional educational approaches, ALEKS dynamically assesses a student's knowledge base, utilizing AI algorithms to gain insights into their strengths and weaknesses across various subjects.

The key feature of ALEKS lies in its adaptability and personalized learning approach. The platform gauges a student's proficiency in specific topics through continuous assessment, identifying knowledge gaps and areas that require reinforcement. This real-time assessment allows ALEKS to tailor the curriculum to each student's unique needs, ensuring a customized learning journey.

Here's how ALEKS works:

ALEKS doesn't rely on standardized testing but instead employs ongoing assessment methods. As students engage with the platform, the AI algorithms analyze their responses to various questions, providing a comprehensive understanding of their mastery levels in different subject areas.

Based on the assessment results, ALEKS dynamically adjusts the learning path for each student. It identifies areas where a student excels and topics that pose challenges, offering a curriculum that specifically targets their knowledge gaps. This personalized approach ensures that students focus on areas requiring improvement while progressing at their optimal pace.

ALEKS understands that each student learns at a different pace. By adapting the curriculum to an individual's proficiency level, the platform facilitates a more efficient learning experience. Students are not held back by a predetermined pace, nor are they rushed through material they haven't mastered.

ALEKS provides instant feedback on students' responses, reinforcing correct answers and offering guidance on areas that need improvement.

This real-time feedback loop enhances the learning process, fostering a deeper understanding of the material.

Educators and students can access detailed reports generated by ALEKS, offering insights into progress, performance, and areas of focus. This data-driven approach enables educators to make informed decisions about their teaching strategies and allows students to track their learning journey.

Smartly

Smartly stands out as an innovative adaptive learning platform tailored specifically for business education. Utilizing cutting-edge AI Smartly transforms the traditional approach to learning by providing a personalized and dynamic educational experience.

Smartly employs an adaptive learning model, which means it tailors educational content to the unique needs and proficiency levels of individual learners. This adaptability is powered by sophisticated AI algorithms that continuously assess and analyze a student's performance.

The platform utilizes AI to customize lessons for each student. By evaluating the learner's strengths and weaknesses, Smartly identifies areas that require reinforcement. This ensures that students receive targeted instruction in subjects where they may need additional support, enhancing the overall effectiveness of the learning experience.

Smartly's adaptive nature allows students to progress efficiently through the curriculum. For concepts they've Hoalready mastered, the platform enables swift advancement, preventing unnecessary repetition and keeping learners engaged. This personalized pace accommodates varying learning speeds, ensuring that each student optimizes their time and focus.

The AI-powered analytics within Smartly offer valuable insights into individual and collective learning patterns. Educators and students can access detailed reports highlighting strengths, improvement areas, and overall progress. These analytics empower educators to make data-driven decisions, adapting their teaching strategies to better meet the needs of their students.

Smartly integrates interactive learning resources, engaging multimedia content, and real-world business scenarios into its lessons. This multifaceted approach, supported by AI, enhances the overall learning experience by providing a rich and immersive educational environment.

Duolingo

Duolingo is a prominent educational technology platform specializing in language learning through an app-based approach. This platform offers a wide range of language courses that users can access for free, making it accessible to learners worldwide. The courses cover various languages and are designed to be interactive, engaging, and effective.

Duolingo proves to be an essential tool for educators on the journey of homeschooling. Its user-friendly interface, diverse language options, and interactive lessons make it a valuable resource for incorporating language learning into the homeschooling curriculum. Duolingo's platform is easily accessible to both educators and students. With a simple and intuitive design, it accommodates users of different age groups and proficiency levels.

The platform offers a wide array of language courses, allowing you to tailor language learning to your students' specific needs and interests. This diversity supports a more personalized and engaging homeschooling experience.

Duolingo's lessons are designed to be interactive and gamified, making the learning process enjoyable for students. This interactive approach helps maintain the interest and motivation of learners, fostering a positive learning environment.

The platform provides tools for tracking students' progress. You can monitor each student's performance, identify areas for improvement, and adjust the learning pace accordingly.

Duolingo's app-based nature offers flexibility regarding when and where students can engage in language learning. This convenience is particularly valuable in a homeschooling setting, where schedules may vary.

Duolingo's commitment to keeping you at the cutting edge of AI is exemplified by its adoption of GPT-4, OpenAI's latest language model. This collaboration places Duolingo among the pioneers offering this state-of-the-art technology to its users, marking a significant stride in the evolution of language education.

OpenAI GPT

OpenAI's GPT technology has gained widespread recognition, notably through applications like ChatGPT, which boasts the fastest-growing user base ever recorded. Building upon this success, GPT-4 has been strategically integrated into select platforms, including the upgraded ChatGPT app and the latest iteration of Microsoft's Bing search engine.

For you, as a language enthusiast and learner, the introduction of GPT-4 brings a new dimension to the language learning experience through Duolingo Max. This represents a noteworthy advancement in the realm of AI-powered language platforms, elevating Duolingo's commitment to providing learners like yourself with cutting-edge tools (Marr, 2023).

Osmo

Osmo is an innovative educational technology that combines physical interaction with digital learning experiences. It consists of a base and a reflector that attaches to a tablet, turning it into an interactive surface. Osmo uses computer vision to track objects and actions in the physical space in front of the tablet, allowing for a seamless blend of hands-on and digital learning.

Osmo provides a range of educational games and activities that cover subjects like math, science, and art. These games are designed to be interactive and engaging, fostering a hands-on learning approach.

Osmo employs AI to adapt to individual students' progress. As students engage in the activities, the system assesses their performance and adjusts the difficulty level to ensure a personalized learning experience. This adaptability caters to the unique needs and abilities of each student.

This tool goes beyond traditional subjects, incorporating elements of art, music, STEM (science, technology, engineering, and mathematics), and special education. This comprehensive approach allows homeschooling educators to provide a well-rounded and interdisciplinary learning experience.

Osmo seamlessly integrates physical and digital components, making it easy for educators to incorporate AI-driven learning into their homeschooling routine. The system is user-friendly, requiring minimal setup, and its intuitive design encourages independent learning.

Osmo's AI capabilities include progress-tracking features, enabling educators to monitor individual student performance. This data-driven insight helps tailor future lessons and provides a clear understanding of each student's strengths and areas that may need more attention.

Interactive Decision Pathway: Personalized AI Learning for Your Students

- Begin with the starting point and consider the hypothetical student's current proficiency in math.
- Use the decision boxes to create pathways based on the student's performance.
- Identify suitable AI tools for various scenarios to tailor the learning experience.

- Add information or specific tools in the placeholders (X and Y) based on your preferences and the needs of your students.
- Customize the pathway to address individual strengths and challenges.

Here are specific AI programs for specific issues the student is facing:

If Struggling With Math

Khan Academy: Offers personalized lessons to address specific weaknesses and continuous assessment for targeted improvement.

If Excelling in Math

Brilliant: It provides challenges to stimulate critical thinking and opportunities for independent exploration.

If Struggling With History

Historypin: It offers Interactive maps and historical photos for immersive learning.

If Excelling in History

Google Arts & Culture: Virtual tours and exhibitions for advanced exploration.

If Struggling With Social Studies

iCivics: Educational games to simplify complex civic concepts.

If Excelling in Social Studies

National Geographic Kids: Engaging multimedia resources for advanced social studies.

If Struggling With Language Arts and Literature

Grammarly: Grammar assistance for language improvement.

If Excelling in Language Arts and Literature

Audible: Audiobooks to enhance literary comprehension.

If Struggling With Physics

PhET Interactive Simulations: Interactive simulations for hands-on physics understanding.

If Excelling in Physics

Wolfram Alpha: Computational knowledge engine for advanced problem-solving.

Additional Tips

- Continuously assess and adapt the AI tools based on student progress.
- Encourage exploration and curiosity by integrating a mix of tools.
- Leverage AI for both foundational concepts and advanced exploration.

In this chapter, we delved into the transformative realm of homeschooling enhanced by AI. From tailored learning materials to adaptive AI-driven games, we explored the myriad benefits AI brings to the homeschooling landscape. The chapter underscored the importance of educators embracing lifelong learning, collaborating with tech experts, and utilizing AI tools to cater to individual student needs.

Key Takeaways

- AI enriches homeschooling by tailoring learning materials and engaging students with educational games.
- Educators must adopt a mindset of lifelong learning to effectively leverage AI in the homeschooling environment.
- Collaboration with tech experts and tracking student progress with AI-powered tools are essential for success.

Putting Ideas into Action

- Explore AI-powered platforms like Duolingo, ALEKS, and Smartly for personalized learning experiences.
- Design decision pathways using AI tools tailored to individual student needs across various subjects.
- Embrace a holistic approach, combining traditional teaching methods with AI-enhanced tools for a balanced homeschooling experience.

As we marvel at the wonders AI has brought to the individualized realms of homeschooling, let's not forget the essence of human interaction. In our next chapter, dive into the world of AI prompts and discover how technology isn't replacing but rather enhancing our age-old art of conversation. Join us on this intriguing journey!

9

THE ART OF AI PROMPTS—A CONVERSATION STARTER

According to a recent survey, half of secondary-level teachers anticipate AI changing education for the better. They believe in a future where education isn't just about knowledge transfer but a dynamic conversation between educators, students, and AI.

As we step into Chapter 9, we're venturing into the captivating world of AI prompts. Have you ever wondered how to make AI not just a tool but a conversation starter? Get ready to master the art of crafting prompts that engage, inspire, and elevate the learning experience.

AI Prompts

An AI prompt, short for "artificial intelligence prompt," refers to a specific input or query provided to an AI system to stimulate a response or generate content. "AI prompts are a powerful tool that uses artificial intelligence (AI). They use machine learning algorithms to learn patterns and associations in data, allowing them to generate more human-like responses" (van der Duim, n.d.).

In the context of education, AI prompts are often used to initiate discussions, encourage critical thinking, and prompt creative responses from students. These prompts can take various forms, including questions, scenarios, or topics, and are designed to engage learners in meaningful interactions with AI-powered systems or tools.

In practice, AI prompts serve as versatile instruments adaptable to various subjects, ranging from history and science to the infusion of creativity in the arts and literature. They transcend the conventional notion of seeking responses; instead, they contribute to fostering an atmosphere of inquisitiveness and dialogue.

Guidelines for Crafting Engaging AI Prompts

Crafting effective AI prompts is crucial, and here are some essential guidelines to assist you in making this task easy:

- **Clarity is key:** Begin with a clear and concise statement. Ambiguity can lead to confusion, and we want our students to focus on the essence of the prompt, not deciphering its meaning.
- **Encourage critical thinking:** Formulate prompts that stimulate critical thinking. Ask questions that require analysis, evaluation, and application of knowledge. This not only challenges students but also nurtures their problem-solving skills.
- **Relate to real-world contexts:** Make the prompts relatable to real-life scenarios. Connecting lessons to the world outside the classroom fosters a deeper understanding and appreciation for the subject matter.
- **Embrace open-ended formats:** Allow room for creativity and diverse responses. Open-ended prompts encourage students to explore various perspectives and express their unique viewpoints, enhancing the richness of the learning experience.
- **Align with learning objectives:** Ensure that your prompts align with specific learning objectives. This strategic alignment ensures that the AI-driven responses contribute meaningfully to the educational goals you've set.
- **Consider personalization:** Leverage AI's capability to personalize prompts based on individual student needs. Tailor questions to their learning pace, interests, and proficiency levels, creating a truly adaptive and supportive learning environment.
- **Feedback integration:** Integrate feedback loops within prompts. Constructive feedback, facilitated by AI, can guide students in refining their understanding and skills, fostering continuous improvement.

Crafting effective AI prompts transcends the mere act of inquiry; it is a deliberate endeavor to spark an insatiable curiosity and foster a profound love for learning. Effective AI prompts serve as catalysts for curiosity. They are designed to awaken the inquisitive nature within students, prompting them to delve deeper into the subject matter. By igniting curiosity, educators set the stage for a journey where each prompt is a steppingstone toward greater knowledge.

The ultimate goal of effective AI prompts is to cultivate lifelong learners. Beyond immediate academic goals, these prompts instill a passion for continuous learning. Students, inspired by thoughtful prompts, develop the mindset of seekers who find joy in unraveling the mysteries of the world around them.

Tailored prompts, driven by AI insights, create personalized learning journeys. Each prompt is uniquely calibrated to the student's pace, interests, and proficiency levels. This customization not only enhances comprehension but also instills a sense of relevance, making learning a personal and meaningful experience.

A Step-By-Step Guide for Creating Effective Prompts

Creating precise and effective prompts for ChatGPT is key to unlocking its full potential for your educational needs. Follow these step-by-step criteria to ensure that your prompts yield valuable and tailored content.

Step 1: Define your objective.

Clearly articulate the goal of your prompt. Are you seeking lesson plan ideas, assistance with specific subjects, or creative resources? A well-defined objective sets the stage for a more targeted and helpful response.

Step 2: Specify the grade level and subject.

Tailor your prompt to your teaching context. Specify the grade level and subject matter to ensure that the generated content aligns with the appropriate curriculum standards and learning objectives.

Step 3: Clarify formatting requirements.

If you have specific formatting preferences for the content (e.g., slides, worksheets, interactive activities), clearly outline these requirements in your prompt. This ensures that the generated materials seamlessly integrate into your teaching resources.

Step 4: Use precise language.

Be explicit and use precise language in your prompt. Clearly state what you're looking for and any specific details or parameters that need to be considered. Avoid ambiguous or open-ended queries to receive more focused responses.

Step 5: Encourage creativity and engagement.

Foster creativity by incorporating prompts that encourage innovative and engaging content. Ask for gamified learning activities, intriguing questions, or unique project ideas to make your teaching materials more dynamic.

Step 6: Request diverse perspectives.

Challenge ChatGPT to provide diverse perspectives on a topic. This is particularly useful for subjects like social studies or literature. Specify if you want viewpoints from different historical figures, authors, or cultural contexts.

Step 7: Incorporate multimedia elements.

Experiment with prompts that involve multimedia elements. If you need visual aids or creative writing prompts, clearly express these requirements. This allows ChatGPT to generate content that aligns with your vision.

Step 8: Iterate and refine.

If the initial response doesn't fully meet your needs, engage in an iterative process. Refine your prompt based on the model's responses to steer the conversation toward the desired outcome. This collaborative approach enhances the effectiveness of the interaction.

Step 9: Check for ethical considerations.

Exercise your professional judgment to evaluate the accuracy and appropriateness of the generated content. Be mindful of ethical considerations and ensure that the information aligns with educational standards and guidelines.

Step 10: Explore new teaching paradigms.

Challenge ChatGPT to brainstorm ideas for incorporating emerging technologies, project-based learning, or collaborative initiatives into your teaching practices. This can be an exciting way to explore new paradigms in education.

Unlocking the Potential: 100 AI Prompts for Educational Enrichment

Here's a curated list of 100 ready-to-use AI prompts designed to cater to various aspects of your teaching journey. Feel free to explore and adapt them for your specific needs.

1. Generate a comprehensive lesson plan for teaching fractions to fifth-grade students.
2. Provide detailed explanations of key scientific concepts suitable for a high school physics class.
3. Create engaging and interactive learning materials for teaching Shakespearean sonnets to a ninth-grade English class.
4. Share insights into multiple historical perspectives on the American Revolution suitable for an eighth-grade history lesson.
5. Craft challenging yet accessible math problems for a seventh-grade class focusing on algebraic expressions.
6. Propose innovative STEM project ideas that integrate technology for a middle school science fair.
7. Generate engaging content about global geography, highlighting unique cultural aspects, for a sixth-grade social studies class.
8. Provide creative writing prompts to stimulate imaginative storytelling for tenth-grade language arts students.
9. Devise coding challenges suitable for a beginner-level high school computer science class.
10. Offer insights into sustainable practices and environmental science experiments for an eleventh-grade class.
11. Create language exercises for an introductory Spanish class, focusing on vocabulary and basic conversation.
12. Develop tools or resources that aid in literary analysis for a twelfth-grade literature class studying classic novels.

13. Formulate a lesson plan on digital citizenship for middle school students, addressing online safety and responsible technology use.
14. Provide step-by-step guides for simple and safe chemistry experiments suitable for a ninth-grade science class.
15. Suggest critical thinking activities for an eighth-grade class, fostering problem-solving skills in mathematics.
16. Create an interactive presentation exploring different art movements and their impact on society for a high school art history class.
17. Generate discussion prompts on civic engagement and current events for a senior-year government class.
18. Help analyze characters in a novel by generating questions and discussion points for a tenth-grade literature class.
19. Propose hands-on physics experiments suitable for a tenth-grade class, emphasizing real-world applications.
20. Explore economic concepts through real-world examples suitable for an eleventh-grade economics class.
21. Provide guidance for an intermediate-level coding project for a high school computer science club.
22. Share insights and resources for teaching comprehensive health education to ninth-grade students.
23. Create math puzzle challenges that enhance logical reasoning skills for a seventh-grade mathematics class.
24. Suggest creative and imaginative art projects for an eighth-grade class, incorporating different mediums.
25. Develop grammar reinforcement exercises for a ninth-grade language arts class focusing on common challenges.
26. Explore digital storytelling ideas using multimedia elements for a tenth-grade media studies class.
27. Provide an overview of major world religions suitable for a twelfth-grade comparative religion class.
28. Design physics simulation challenges to reinforce theoretical concepts for an advanced eleventh-grade physics class.
29. Offer insights into current geopolitical issues for a senior-year international relations class.

30. Inspire ideas for a capstone project in any subject area for graduating high school students.
31. Devise a project that raises environmental awareness by integrating science, art, and community engagement for a middle school class.
32. Explore various literary genres, providing resources and discussion prompts for a ninth-grade literature class.
33. Create a mathematical modeling task that simulates real-world scenarios for an advanced tenth-grade mathematics class.
34. Propose ideas for building a digital art portfolio, incorporating diverse styles and techniques for an eleventh-grade art class.
35. Develop a coding boot camp module for high school students, covering fundamental programming concepts.
36. Design a global economics simulation that allows students to navigate economic challenges for a twelfth-grade economics class.
37. Reinforce fundamental chemistry concepts through interactive exercises for a ninth-grade science class.
38. Generate debate topics based on historical events, encouraging critical analysis for a senior-year history class.
39. Facilitate inquiry-based learning in physics with hands-on experiments for a tenth-grade science class.
40. Create public speaking challenges that enhance communication skills for a senior-year communications class.
41. Develop literature review assignments that guide students in researching and analyzing literary topics for a twelfth-grade English class.
42. Craft interactive algebra lessons using visual aids and real-world examples for an eighth-grade mathematics class.
43. Initiate a discussion on coding ethics, exploring the ethical implications of technology for a high school computer science class.
44. Generate engaging quizzes on world geography, covering diverse regions and cultures for a middle school social studies class.
45. Facilitate a health and wellness project integrating physical and mental health components for a tenth-grade health education class.

46. Organize a creative writing workshop with prompts and exercises for enhancing narrative skills in an eleventh-grade language arts class.
47. Create animations explaining complex physics principles, aiding understanding in a ninth-grade physics class.
48. Debunk common science myths and misconceptions, fostering scientific literacy in an eighth-grade science class.
49. Explore cultural diversity through literature, highlighting works from various regions for a tenth-grade literature class.
50. Illustrate how mathematics is applied in everyday life, providing relatable examples for a seventh-grade math class.
51. Conduct a workshop on digital media literacy, guiding students on discerning credible sources for research in a twelfth-grade media studies class.
52. Propose creative ideas for a science fair project, incorporating innovation and experimentation for a middle school science class.
53. Initiate an art history exhibition project, allowing students to curate and present their insights in a tenth-grade art history class.
54. Organize a mathematics puzzle marathon, challenging students with a series of puzzles for an advanced eighth-grade math class.
55. Craft interactive biology lessons with virtual simulations for exploring biological concepts in a ninth-grade science class.
56. Facilitate a group project for literary analysis, encouraging collaboration and critical thinking in an eleventh-grade literature class.
57. Guide students in coding projects with a social impact, addressing community needs for a high school computer science club.
58. Initiate podcast discussions on geopolitical events, providing insights and analysis for a senior-year international relations class.
59. Challenge students with a digital storytelling project, combining multimedia elements for a ninth-grade media studies class.

60. Explore the science of cooking through culinary experiments, connecting chemistry and physics for an eleventh-grade home economics class.
61. Develop an interactive historical timeline using AI, highlighting key events and their global impact, for a tenth-grade history class.
62. Guide students in analyzing environmental science data sets, fostering data literacy in an eleventh-grade science class.
63. Organize a panel discussion on the ethical implications of AI, involving experts and students for a senior-year philosophy class.
64. Explore the intersection of mathematics and art, encouraging students to create geometric artworks for an eighth-grade art class.
65. Curate a virtual science museum tour using AI technology, allowing students to explore exhibits from different scientific disciplines for a ninth-grade science class.
66. Analyze the portrayal of technology in literature, exploring its impact on storytelling for an eleventh-grade language arts class.
67. Engage students in a digital civics project, prompting them to research and address societal issues using AI for a senior-year civics class.
68. Investigate the role of AI in preserving and promoting language diversity by connecting technology with linguistic studies in a tenth-grade linguistics class.
69. Conduct a space exploration simulation, using AI data to create realistic scenarios for a middle school astronomy class.
70. Explore AI's role in music composition, guiding students to analyze and create AI-generated music for an eighth-grade music class.
71. Present philosophical dilemmas related to AI, encouraging students to reflect on moral and ethical considerations for a senior-year ethics class.
72. Host a data journalism workshop, empowering students to use AI tools for analyzing and visualizing data in news reporting for a journalism class.

73. Initiate a digital wellness campaign, prompting students to create and promote strategies for healthy technology use in a ninth-grade health education class.
74. Explore AI applications in language learning, recommending tools and methods for language acquisition for a tenth-grade foreign language class.
75. Challenge students to write science fiction stories envisioning the future of AI, blending creativity with technological foresight for an eleventh-grade creative writing class.
76. Integrate AI in archaeological research, guiding students to use technology for data analysis and interpretation in a senior-year archaeology class.
77. Task students with developing a math problem-solving app using AI algorithms for an eighth-grade computer science class.
78. Explore the integration of AI in sustainable design projects, fostering creativity and environmental awareness in a tenth-grade design and technology class.
79. Encourage students to code projects that address social issues, linking technology skills with community impact for a senior-year computer science club.
80. Create a virtual reality history tour using AI, immersing students in historical events for a ninth-grade history class.
81. Guide students in using AI to enhance poetry analysis, exploring the intersection of technology and literature in an eleventh-grade literature class.
82. Challenge students to design a digital health-tracking app using AI, promoting personal wellness in a senior-year health education class.
83. Develop interactive physics simulations using AI, aiding students in visualizing complex concepts for a tenth-grade physics class.
84. Analyze the impact of AI on the gaming industry, exploring technological advancements and ethical considerations for a senior-year business studies class.
85. Engage students in geographical data mapping, utilizing AI tools to analyze and visualize spatial information for a ninth-grade geography class.

86. Explore the intersection of AI and human psychology, guiding students to understand how technology influences behavior in an eleventh-grade psychology class.
87. Conduct a digital citizenship workshop, prompting students to explore responsible and ethical technology use for a senior-year social studies class.
88. Encourage students to advocate for AI by enhancing accessibility, researching, and presenting solutions in a tenth-grade advocacy class.
89. Organize a virtual reality art exhibition using AI, allowing students to showcase digital artworks for an eighth-grade art class.
90. Explore the application of AI in wildlife conservation, guiding students to understand the role of technology in protecting biodiversity in a ninth-grade environmental science class.
91. Task students with developing a language translation app using AI algorithms, promoting cross-cultural communication for a tenth-grade foreign language class.
92. Encourage students to explore the creative aspects of AI in mathematics, fostering innovative problem-solving in an eleventh-grade mathematics class.
93. Explore the integration of AI in digital storytelling, guiding students to create multimedia narratives for a senior-year media studies class.
94. Engage students in a sports analytics project using AI, analyzing performance data for strategic insights in a tenth-grade sports science class.
95. Develop interactive biology lab simulations using AI, allowing students to conduct virtual experiments for a ninth-grade biology class.
96. Explore the use of AI-driven language learning games, promoting interactive and engaging language acquisition in an eighth-grade language arts class.
97. Conduct a mathematics and cryptography workshop, guiding students to explore the connections between mathematics and data security in a tenth-grade computer science class.

98. Integrate AI in astrophysics research, guiding students to analyze astronomical data for a senior-year astrophysics class.
99. Encourage collaboration between digital arts and AI, guiding students to create innovative multimedia projects for an eleventh-grade digital arts class.
100. Guide students in incorporating AI technology into their science fair projects, fostering innovation and creativity for a senior-year science class.

Crafting Engaging AI Prompts for Students

As an educator, you wield the power to ignite curiosity and fuel learning journeys through well-crafted AI prompts. One critical aspect of this craft is tailoring questions to the age of your students. Why does it matter?

In the world of education, confusion is the nemesis of curiosity. Crafting questions that match the age group ensures that students are intrigued, not overwhelmed. Questions should spark curiosity, leading them on a quest for knowledge, not leave them lost in a maze of complexity.

Age-appropriate questions invite active participation. They empower students to express their thoughts, share insights, and contribute meaningfully to discussions.

Success breeds confidence. By tailoring prompts to the age group, you set the stage for success. Students feel capable of tackling challenges within their grasp, fostering a positive learning environment where each small victory becomes a steppingstone.

The teenage mind grapples with different questions than the curious musings of a young learner. Age-appropriate prompts resonate with the realities students face, connecting learning to their lived experiences and making it relevant.

As you generate prompts, it is crucial to consider the age group you are targeting. Some prompts may be below the appropriate age level for your students, while others might be too advanced, potentially hindering the goal of enhanced learning. Ensuring that prompts are well-curated and specifically tailored to the age group is essential for achieving the desired outcomes in the learning process.

Interactive Element: Crafting Effective ChatGPT Prompts

Now, it's time for you to take the reins and become the architect of engaging AI prompts! Let's delve into the art of crafting effective ChatGPT prompts, a skill that can elevate your interactions with AI and enhance your overall teaching experience.

- Start with a generic, vague example: "Tell me about teaching methods."
- Now, counter with a refined version: "Explain active learning strategies for middle school math."

Your Turn

Think of a broad educational topic that intrigues you. Once you have it in mind, your challenge is to refine and sharpen it for greater precision. Aim for clarity and specificity in your prompt. This exercise isn't just about creating prompts; it's about honing a skill that can significantly enhance your classroom instruction and communication.

As we wrap up this chapter on the art of AI prompts, remember that the key to effective engagement lies in your ability to frame questions that inspire curiosity and ignite a passion for learning. Take a moment to reflect on the prompts you've encountered and created—the gateways to valuable insights and knowledge.

Now, it's time to turn insights into action. Experiment with crafting your own prompts, tailoring them to your unique educational context. Challenge yourself to refine and clarify, discovering the power that precision holds in the world of AI-driven conversations.

In the upcoming chapter, we'll explore a crucial facet of integrating AI into education—maintaining the human touch. As we become more proficient in navigating the landscape of AI, let's ensure that the warmth, empathy, and genuine connections in our classrooms remain steadfast.

Join us in the next part as we delve into strategies to harmonize technological advancements with the essential human elements of teaching and learning.

10

AI AND THE HUMAN TOUCH—STRIKING A BALANCE IN THE CLASSROOM

Did you know that while AI can analyze data patterns and provide feedback, it can't recognize the subtle emotional nuances in a struggling student's face or the spark in their eyes when they finally understand a concept? How can educators balance the efficiency of AI with the irreplaceable human touch?

In this chapter, we'll unravel the profound understanding that AI, while a remarkable tool, can never replace the quintessential human touch in teaching. It's not about choosing one over the other but discovering the synergy between these elements to create a harmonious and effective educational experience.

The Integral Role of Human Emotion and Intuition in Education

In the world of education, emotions, intuition, and touch are essential components, much like a conductor leading an orchestra. The essence lies in the subtle skill of comprehending and addressing the individual emotional experiences of our students. This skill unlocks the genuine magic of teaching, creating a meaningful connection that goes beyond the surface.

Emotion is a vital and intrinsic aspect of the educational landscape, weaving through every interaction, lesson, and shared moment within the classroom. As an educator, you are not just a provider of information; you are a facilitator of emotional experiences that significantly impact your students. Emotions, both yours and those of your students, create a fruitful connection, engagement, and understanding.

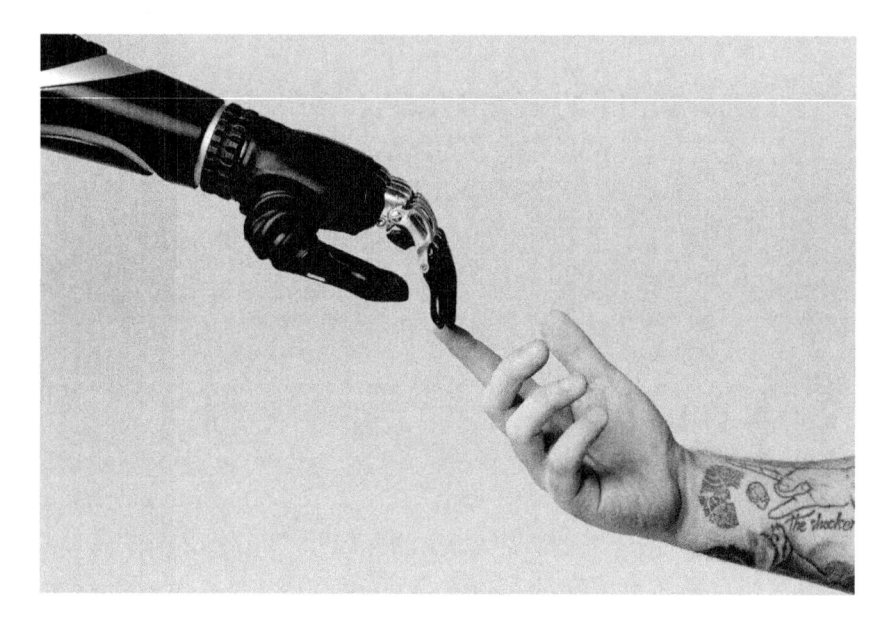

Consider the joy that lights up a student's face when they grasp a challenging concept, the empathy you feel when a student faces a personal struggle, or the shared enthusiasm during a collaborative learning activity. These emotional nuances are not distractions, but rather the essence of the teaching and learning process.

Recognizing and acknowledging emotions in an educational setting is a powerful tool for building trust and rapport. It allows you to create a safe and supportive environment where students feel seen, valued, and understood. Emotion is the fuel that propels the educational journey, making lessons memorable, fostering a positive classroom culture, and inspiring a genuine passion for learning.

Intuition in the context of education is a nuanced and instinctive understanding that teachers develop over time through experience and observation. It involves the ability to read between the lines, discern unspoken cues, and make insightful judgments about students' needs, emotions, and learning styles.

In the classroom, intuition allows you to go beyond the surface, anticipating challenges, recognizing individual strengths, and adapting your teaching methods accordingly. It's an unspoken language that teachers use to connect with their students on a deeper level, fostering an environment where learning is not just about acquiring knowledge but also about understanding and addressing the unique aspects of each student's journey. Intuition, therefore, becomes an indispensable guide for educators, helping them navigate the complexities of the human experience within the realm of education.

Blaire Lent, the proprietor and primary instructor at The Complete Student in Beaufort, South Carolina, runs a small, private educational facility catering to homeschooling middle and high school students. With a focus on enrichment and online academics, many students enrolled here have struggled with a sense of belonging in traditional school settings, prompting their parents to seek a more personalized and supportive environment. Lent shares a similar perspective on the significance of touch, expressing that she deliberately incorporates gestures like patting students on the back or placing a hand on their shoulders. She believes this approach serves multiple purposes, including aiding in directing and maintaining attention and serving as a reminder to students that she is a genuine human presence ready to support them. In her view, incorporating touch is a means for both students and teachers to reintroduce a sense of humanity into the teaching process (Miranda, 2016).

AI's Complementary Role in Teaching

The synergy between AI and the human teacher is a testament to the evolving landscape of education, where technology enhances rather than supplants the invaluable role you play.

AI, with its ability to analyze vast datasets and adapt swiftly, becomes your ally in tailoring learning experiences. It identifies individual student needs, suggests personalized resources, and assists in crafting educational journeys that resonate with diverse learning styles.

AI streamlines routine tasks such as grading, attendance tracking, and data analysis, allowing you to channel your energy into more impactful facets of teaching—connecting with students, fostering creativity, and inspiring intellectual curiosity.

AI augments your creative capacities. By automating certain processes, it provides you with more time to design innovative and engaging lesson plans. Think of it as a collaborator, offering suggestions and insights to fuel your pedagogical creativity.

Strategies to Ensure AI Remains a Tool, not a Replacement

From the word go, we emphasized that AI is here and it's here to stay, and it is upon us to ensure it remains a tool and not our replacement as educators. Here are strategies to ensure this is achieved:

- Create a nurturing classroom atmosphere that places a premium on human connections. Although AI plays a significant role in several educational facets, the true essence of education is embedded in the genuine relationships cultivated with your students. Actively participate in meaningful discussions, exhibit empathetic listening skills, and remain finely attuned to the emotional subtleties that extend beyond the grasp of AI. Remember, the heart of teaching lies in the authentic and personal connections you forge with your students.
- Present AI as a collaborative ally in the educational journey. Encourage students to collaborate, exchange ideas, and participate in group activities. While AI can enhance these interactions by providing varied perspectives and resources, it's essential to recognize that the true essence of collaboration is inherently human. Emphasize the idea that, while AI can be a valuable tool, the collaborative spirit remains rooted in the human experience of working together, sharing insights, and engaging collectively in the learning process.
- Utilize AI to craft personalized learning experiences, customizing educational paths according to individual needs. Nevertheless, retain your role as the conductor of this

personalized journey. Interpret insights generated by AI and adapt them to meet the distinctive requirements of each student, ensuring a finely tuned and tailored educational experience.
- Emphasize critical thinking and problem-solving skills. While AI excels in data analysis and pattern recognition, nurturing the ability to question, analyze, and synthesize information is a distinctly human skill. Guide students in developing a critical lens to navigate the wealth of information AI provides.
- Instill ethical considerations in the use of technology. Teach students the responsible and mindful utilization of AI tools, emphasizing the importance of integrity, privacy, and digital citizenship. Cultivate a sense of responsibility that transcends the capabilities of AI.
- Stay informed and continuously develop your teaching skills. Attend workshops, engage in professional development programs, and remain at the forefront of educational trends. This proactive approach ensures that you remain the driving force behind educational innovation.

Balancing AI and Human Intervention Worksheet

Instructions: List down the tasks you believe can be efficiently managed by AI in one column. On the other hand, jot down those tasks that you feel require the warmth, intuition, and personal touch only a human can provide.

The Human-AI Balance Sheet

Tasks for AI

Tasks for human touch

- Grading multiple-choice quizzes
- Comforting a distressed student
- Data analysis for student trends
- Providing personalized feedback
- Managing lesson scheduling
- Fostering a sense of belonging

LEADING THE WAY IN AI EDUCATION

Now that you've gained the knowledge and confidence to skillfully navigate the world of AI in education, it's your chance to lead the way and guide other readers towards the same enlightenment.

You've acquired the skills and insights to steer the AI education boat with confidence, and there are fellow educators out there eager to follow your course. Share your newfound wisdom and let them know where they can access the same invaluable assistance.

Here's how you can make a difference:

- Share Your Review: If this book has empowered you in your educational journey, consider leaving a review. Your words can inspire others to embark on the AI education voyage.
- Pass the Torch: Recommend this book to your fellow educators, friends, and colleagues who are seeking to embrace AI in their teaching practices.
- Stay Connected: Keep the dialogue alive by engaging with educational communities, online forums, or local teacher networks. Share your experiences and exchange ideas about AI in the classroom.
- Be a Mentor: Offer your guidance and mentorship to those seeking to explore AI's potential in education. Your expertise can be a guiding light for others.

Thank you for your dedication to advancing education through AI. Your commitment is shaping the future of learning and empowering educators worldwide.

Let's continue to skillfully navigate the AI education boat and lead the way to a brighter future!

-With gratitude, Teach Wise Publications

To leave your review, simply scan the QR code below:

REFLECTION SPACE

Having listed the tasks, how do you envision balancing AI and human intervention in your future classroom?

- _____
- _____
- _____
- _____
- _____
- _____
- _____
- _____
- _____
- _____
- _____
- _____
- _____
- _____
- _____
- _____
- _____
- _____
- _____
- _____
- _____
- _____
- _____
- _____
- _____
- _____
- _____
- _____
- _____
- _____

As we conclude this enlightening chapter, let's reflect on the symbiotic dance of AI and human connection in education. Now armed with insights to harness AI as a powerful tool, it's time for you, the educator, to take center stage. Embrace the technological future while preserving the timeless human touch in your teaching.

Having gained a profound insight into the role of AI and the invaluable essence of human connection, we now move toward the conclusion of our exploration. As educators navigating the digital era, always keep in mind the distinctive value you contribute to the classroom. Utilize AI as a tool to enhance your influence, not substitute it.

CONCLUSION

In the evolving landscape of education, this comprehensive journey through the pages of our book has shed light on the dynamic relationship between educators and AI. Our primary message resonates with the ever-changing nature of teaching and learning: Leverage technology not as a replacement but as a powerful tool to augment your teaching capabilities. As educators in the digital era, you hold a unique position to shape the future of learning by combining the strengths of AI with the irreplaceable human touch.

Throughout the chapters, we've explored the myriad ways AI can be harnessed to streamline administrative tasks, personalize learning experiences, and provide valuable insights. Yet, amidst technological advancements, we consistently emphasize the essence of human connection, intuition, and emotion in education. The interplay between technology and personal touch creates a synergistic approach that fosters meaningful and effective learning environments.

At the heart of this transformative journey lies a singular key takeaway: Educators are architects of the future, shaping the evolving landscape of education by leveraging the power of AI as a strategic ally. The book underscores that AI is not a replacement for the human touch but a dynamic tool, offering a multitude of opportunities to enhance and amplify the impact of educators.

Throughout the chapters, the narrative weaves insights, strategies, and interactive elements, guiding educators to integrate AI seamlessly into their teaching practices. The overarching message resonates with the importance of balance—balancing the efficiencies of AI with the irreplaceable qualities of human connection, intuition, and empathy.

As educators navigate the digital era, the book empowers them to embrace AI with confidence, providing a roadmap to harness its capabilities effectively. It emphasizes the significance of remaining proactive rather than reactive, encouraging educators to stay informed, adopt innovative practices, and cultivate a future-ready mindset.

In essence, the book positions educators as the driving force behind the integration of AI in education, urging them to wield technology as a tool for empowerment, personalization, and progress. It calls upon educators to embark on this journey with purpose, recognizing the symbiotic relationship between human expertise and technological advancements. The key takeaway is a call to action—a call for educators to lead the way, ensuring that the educational landscape is not just shaped by AI but guided by the wisdom, compassion, and skill of dedicated educators.

The United States, a trailblazer in educational innovation, has embraced the transformative potential of AI to redefine teaching and learning experiences. AI integration in American classrooms has witnessed a surge, with intelligent tutoring systems, virtual and augmented reality, and data analytics leading the charge. Intelligent tutoring systems powered by AI algorithms provide personalized support and feedback, adapting to individual learning needs. Virtual and augmented reality create immersive learning environments, fostering engagement and interactivity. Data analytics, a linchpin of AI implementation, enables evidence-based decision-making by analyzing vast student datasets.

In our exploration, we encounter success stories that echo the transformative impact of AI. The Summit Learning Program, a collaboration between Summit Public Schools and Facebook, stands out. This AI-powered personalized learning platform tailors education to each student's pace and style, leading to increased engagement, improved academic performance, and better college preparedness.

Carnegie Learning's AI-driven math curriculum is another beacon of success. This adaptive learning program employs AI algorithms to assess knowledge gaps and provide targeted instruction, resulting in significant improvements in students' math proficiency and problem-solving skills.

The popularity of AI-powered language learning platforms, such as Duolingo, in American classrooms signifies a paradigm shift. These platforms, utilizing AI algorithms, offer personalized language instruction, empowering students to learn at their own pace and track progress effectively (Teachflow, 2022).

As you reflect on the insights gained from these pages, remember the transformative power you wield as an educator. Embrace AI not as a disruptor but as an ally, an invaluable companion in your mission to nurture the minds of the future. Your expertise, empathy, and personal touch are indispensable components of the educational journey. Use AI judiciously, letting it amplify your impact without overshadowing the human connection that makes education truly impactful.

Now, with a deepened understanding of the harmonious relationship between educators and AI, we embark on the conclusion of our shared journey. It's a culmination of insights, strategies, and reflections aimed at empowering you to navigate the evolving landscape of education with confidence and purpose.

As the curtain falls on this exploration of AI in education, let us not merely reflect but propel ourselves forward. The evolution of AI beckons, and with it, the call for continuous learning and adaptation. Dedicate time to regular professional development, whether through courses, webinars, or conferences. The horizon of AI in education is expansive, and staying informed will ensure you remain at the forefront. Embrace the synergy of human expertise and technological innovation and let your journey into the AI-infused realm of education be one of perpetual growth and empowerment. The future is ours to shape, and with each stride, may we stride confidently into the boundless possibilities that lie ahead.

Conclusion

We value your opinion! If you found this book helpful and informative, please consider leaving a review. Your feedback is essential in helping us improve and provide valuable content. Thank you for being part of our learning community!

BIBLIOGRAPHY

Adarsh. (2023, May 14). *AI vs. traditional education: the battle for the classroom of the future.* Ideal Adarsh Tech Lover. https://idealadarsh.com/ai-vs-traditional-education-the-battle-for-the-classroom-of-the-future/

Alecia. (2023, May 11). *5 incredible ways to use AI for homeschooling: benefits & tools.* No Stress Homeschooling. https://nostresshomeschooling.com/ai-for-homeschooling-tips-and-tools/

Asokan, A. (2019). *Facial recognition use triggers GDPR fine.* Bank Info Security. https://www.bankinfosecurity.com/facial-recognition-use-triggers-gdpr-fine-a-12991

Baker, R. S., & Hawn, A. (2021). Algorithmic bias in education. *International Journal of Artificial Intelligence in Education, 32*(32). https://doi.org/10.1007/s40593-021-00285-9

Centre For Teaching Excellence. (n.d.). *Chatbots and artificial intelligence in education.* Center for Teaching Excellence. https://teach.ufl.edu/resource-library/chatbots-and-artificial-intelligence-in-education/

Coursera. (n.d.). *Most popular online courses: Coursera anniversary collection.* Coursera. https://www.coursera.org/collections/popular-online-courses-coursera-anniversary

Digital Learning Institute. (2023, May 9). *6 myths about AI in learning.* Digital Learning Institute. https://www.digitallearninginstitute.com/blog/myths-ai-learning/

Duim, H. V. D. (n.d.). *What you need to know about AI prompts.* HackerNoon. https://hackernoon.com/what-you-need-to-know-about-ai-prompts

Education World. (2013). *How to use Edmodo in the classroom.* Education World. https://www.educationworld.com/a_tech/how-educators-can-use-edmodo.shtml

Eklavvya Assessments. (2023, February 21). *31 incredible AI tools for education you need to try right now!* Splashgain Technology Solutions. https://www.eklavvya.com/blog/ai-edtech-tools/

Falcon, S., Admiraal, W., & Leon, J. (2023). Teachers' engaging messages and the relationship with students' performance and teachers' enthusiasm. *Learning and Instruction, 86*, 101750. https://doi.org/10.1016/j.learninstruc.2023.101750

Frąckiewicz, M. (2023a, July 17). *The role of AI in streamlining administrative tasks in education.* TS2 SPACE. https://ts2.space/en/the-role-of-ai-in-streamlining-administrative-tasks-in-education/#gsc.tab=0

Frąckiewicz, M. (2023b, August 28). *How AI is changing the way we assess student performance.* TS2 SPACE. https://ts2.space/en/how-ai-is-changing-the-way-we-assess-student-performance/#gsc.tab=0

Gates, B. (n.d.). In Brandon, J. (n.d.). *25 quotes from Bill Gates on how to succeed.* Inc.Africa.com. https://www.incafrica.com/library/john-brandon-25-of-the-best-bill-gates-quotes-on-success

George, A. (2023, May 31). *The importance of Artificial Intelligence in education for all students.* Language Magazine. https://www.languagemagazine.com/2023/05/31/the-importance-of-artificial-intelligence-in-education-for-all-students/#:~:text=AI%20can%20also%20help%20teachers

Gillette, H. (2022, December 9). *The only constant is change: what to make of this.* Psych Central. https://psychcentral.com/lib/the-only-constant-is-change#what-it-means

Graham, G. (2023, April 9). *Revolutionizing homeschooling: the AI advantage*. Future School AI Homeschool. https://www.futureschoolai.com/blog/revolutionizing-homeschooling-the-ai-advantage

Guan, C., Mou, J., & Jiang, Z. (2020). Artificial intelligence innovation in education: A twenty-year data-driven historical analysis. *International Journal of Innovation Studies*, 4(4), 134–147. https://doi.org/10.1016/j.ijis.2020.09.001

Gürkan, I., Mehmet, E., & Serkan, Y. (2018). Analysis of use of virtual reality technologies in history education: a case study. *Asian Journal of Education and Training*, 4(2), 62–69. https://doi.org/10.20448/journal.522.2018.42.62.69

Heraclitus (n.d.). In ArapahoeTim. (2020, September 9). *The only constant in life is change. - Heraclitus*. Arapahoe Libraries. https://arapahoelibraries.org/blogs/post/the-only-constant-in-life-is-change-heraclitus/

Kimmons, R. (2020). Lifelong Learning. In *K–12 Educational Technology Handbook*. EdTech Books. https://edtechbooks.org/k12handbook/lifelong_learning

King, M. L. (n.d.). *Martin Luther King quotes*. Brainy Quote. https://www.brainyquote.com/quotes/martin_luther_king_jr_402936

Klay, A. (2010, October 5). *The best way to invent the future is to predict it*. PARC. https://www.parc.com/blog/the-best-way-to-invent-the-future-is-to-predict-it-2/

Kurtz, H., Lloyd, S., Harwin, A., & Osher, M. (2018). *School leaders and technology: results from a national survey*. ERIC. https://eric.ed.gov/?id=ED586959

Larkin, Z. (2022, November 16). *AI bias - what is it and how to avoid it?* Levity.ai. https://levity.ai/blog/ai-bias-how-to-avoid

Llywodraeth Cymru Welsh Government. (2020). *A teacher's guide to the general data protection regulation and what it means for your school*. Llywodraeth Cymru Llywodraeth Cymru Welsh Government. https://hwb.gov.wales/keeping-safe-online/resources/a-teachers-guide-to-the-general-data-protection-regulation-and-what-it-means-for-your-school

Marr, B. (2023). *The amazing ways Duolingo is using AI and GPT-4*. Future Tech Trends. https://www.linkedin.com/pulse/amazing-ways-duolingo-using-ai-gpt-4-bernard-marr/

Miranda. (2016, October 16). *Connections: the value of touch in the classroom*. The Indigo Teacher. http://theindigoteacher.com/connections-the-value-of-touch-in-the-classroom/

Ouyang, F., Wu, M., Zheng, L., Zhang, L., Jiao, P. (2023). Integration of artificial intelligence performance prediction and learning analytics to improve student learning in online engineering course. *ProQuest, 20*, 4. https://doi.org/10.1186/s41239-022-00372-4

Piech, C., & Einstein, L. (2020). *A vision of AI for joyful education*. Scientific American Blog Network. https://blogs.scientificamerican.com/observations/a-vision-of-ai-for-joyful-education/

Plitnichenko, L. (2020, May 30). *5 main roles of artificial intelligence in education*. ELearning Industry. https://elearningindustry.com/5-main-roles-artificial-intelligence-in-education

Santhika, E. (2023, April 11). *Embracing AI in NZ: transforming the educational landscape*. OpenGov Asia. https://opengovasia.com/embracing-ai-in-nz-transforming-the-educational-landscape/

Santosh, K. (2023). *The rise of education and AI: will robots replace teachers?* LinkedIn Corporation. https://www.linkedin.com/pulse/rise-education-ai-robots-replace-teachers-santosh-k/

Smith, L. (2022, May 23). *Moving on from standardized tests to AI: helping students and teachers in real-time*. Emerging Education Technologies. https://www.emergingedtech.com/2022/05/end-standardized-tests-ai-helping-students-teachers-real-time/

Socrates. (n.d.). *Socrates quotes*. Goodreads. https://www.goodreads.com/quotes/69267-education-is-the-kindling-of-a-flame-not-the-filling

Talari, S. (2018, May 25). *6 AI subscriptions to keep you informed*. Medium. https://becominghuman.ai/6-ai-subscriptions-to-keep-you-informed-4cfc6cb024a

Teachflow. (2022, November 1). *AI in education: global success stories unveiled*. Teachflow. https://teachflow.ai/ai-in-education-global-success-stories-unveiled/

The Journal of Artificial Intelligence Research. (2023). *Artificial Intelligence research in education*. The Journal of Artificial Intelligence Research. https://www.jair.org/index.php/jair

The Legal Intelligencer. (2023). *Data matters—risks and best practices for use of generative AI*. Blank Rome LLP. https://www.blankrome.com/publications/data-matters-risks-and-best-practices-use-generative-ai

Thompson, W. E. and N. (2023, August 27). *Teachers turn to AI to make workload more manageable, chart lesson plans*. CP24. https://www.cp24.com/mobile/news/teachers-turn-to-ai-to-make-workload-more-manageable-chart-lesson-plans-1.6536738

University of San Diego. (2021). *43 examples of artificial intelligence in education*. University of San Diego. https://onlinedegrees.sandiego.edu/artificial-intelligence-education/

Walch, K. (2018, July 9). *20 AI-focused podcasts to listen to*. AI & Data Today. https://www.aidatatoday.com/20-ai-focused-podcasts-to-listen-to/

Image References

Bertollazi, I. (n.d.). *Photo neon* [Image]. Pexels. https://www.pexels.com/photo/neon-signage-2681319/

Cameron, J. M. (n.d.). *Woman in pink top* [Image]. Pexels. https://www.pexels.com/photo/woman-in-pink-shirt-sitting-by-the-table-while-smiling-4143791/

Cottonbro.studio. (n.d.-a). *Bionic hand and human hand* [Image]. Pexels. https://www.pexels.com/photo/bionic-hand-and-human-hand-finger-pointing-6153354/

Cottonbro.studio. (n.d.-b). *Woman in grey hijab* [Image]. Pexels. https://www.pexels.com/photo/woman-in-gray-hijab-sitting-on-couch-4620862/

Cottonbro.studio. (n.d.-c). *Woman using VR* [Image]. Pexels. https://www.pexels.com/photo/a-woman-in-a-tank-top-using-a-vr-headset-8721318/

Danilivechi, O. (n.d.). *Two men looking at laptop* [Image]. Pexels. https://www.pexels.com/photo/two-men-looking-at-a-laptop-4974920/

Darmel, A. (n.d.). *Two girls having an online class while writing* [Image]. Pexels. https://www.pexels.com/photo/two-girls-having-an-online-class-while-writing-9037328/

Fauxels. (n.d.). *Group of people discussing using Macbook* [Image]. In Pexels. https://www.pexels.com/photo/top-view-photo-of-group-of-people-using-macbook-while-discussing-3182773/

Holmes, K. (n.d.). *Cheerful teacher* [Image]. Pexels. https://www.pexels.com/photo/cheerful-black-teacher-with-diverse-schoolkids-5905918/

ABOUT THE AUTHOR

Teach Wise Publications is dedicated to empowering educators with AI insights! Your go-to source for innovative AI resources.